OUR MARYL

BOOK
THIRTY-NINE

# HARDING FAMILIES

William Neal Hurley, Jr.

HERITAGE BOOKS, INC.

W.N. Hurley, Jr.
9423 Eagleton Lane
Montgomery Village, Maryland 20886

Published 2002 by

HERITAGE BOOKS, INC.
1540E Pointer Ridge Place
Bowie, Maryland 20716

1-800-398-7709
www.heritagebooks.com

ISBN 0-7884-2239-1

# OUR MARYLAND HERITAGE

## Book Thirty-nine

## Harding Families

Primarily of Montgomery County, but including Family members found in other counties of the State.

## ALSO BY W. N. HURLEY, JR.

*Available from the publisher: Heritage Books, Inc.*

*Neikirk-Newkirk-Nikirk, Volume 1, Revised*
*Neikirk-Newkirk-Nikirk, Volume 2*
*Hurley Families in America, Volumes 1 & 2, Revised*
*John William Hines 1600, And His Descendants, Revised*
*Maddox, A Southern Maryland Family*
*Pratt Families of Virginia and Associated Families*
*Lowder Families in America*
*1850 Census of Montgomery County, Maryland*
*1860 Census of Montgomery County, Maryland*
*1870 Census of Montgomery County, Maryland*
*1880 Census of Montgomery County, Maryland*

*1900 Census of Montgomery County, Maryland*
**Winner 2001 Norris Harris Prize, Maryland Historical Society**
*"Best compilation of genealogical source records of Maryland"*

*Our Maryland Heritage Series:*

*Book 1: Fry*
*Book 2: Walker*
*Book 3: Fulks*
*Book 4: Watkins*
*Book 5: King*
*Book 6: Burdette*
*Book 7: Soper*
*Book 8: Brandenburg*
*Book 9: Purdum*
*Book 10: Perry*
*Book 11: Stottlemyer*
*Book 12: Browning*
*Book 13: Miles*
*Book 14: Lewis*
*Book 15: Warfield*
*Book 16: White*
*Book 17: Mullinix/Mullineaux*
*Book 18: Young*
*Book 19: Bowman and Gue*
*Book 20: Trundle and Allied Families*
*Book 21: Fisher and Beckwith*
*Book 22: Davis*
*Book 23: Etchison*
*Book 24: Holland*
*Book 25: Ricketts*
*Book 26: Trail*
*Book 27: Rabbitt*
*Book 28: Baker*
*Book 29: Selby*
*Book 30: Ward*
*Book 31: Hays and Gott*
*Book 32: Waters*
*Book 33: Griffith*
*Book 34: Hawkins*
*Book 35: Benson*
*Book 36: Ray*
*Book 37: Higgins*
*Book 38: Shaw*

# INTRODUCTION

This is the thirty-ninth book in our series of studies of families primarily found in Montgomery County, but including some records from other nearby counties and elsewhere. We began the study with the goal of providing information about the Harding families generally found in Montgomery County, as listed in the various census returns from 1850 to 1900, and expanded it to include information from a number of other sources.

The data contained in this report is not intended to be an all-inclusive genealogy of the family under study. It was prepared from information found in a variety of sources, including records found at the library of the Montgomery County Historical Society, such as family files, church and cemetery records, obituary collections, and the published books and abstracts held by the library in their research collection; as well as the personal library of the author, and earlier family studies. We have expanded that by somewhat limited personal research in the courthouse of Montgomery County, and available census records, as well as published reports, histories and family genealogies of related families. We have not confirmed all of the data by personal examination of contemporary records, and can not, therefore, vouch for its accuracy in all cases. Others are, of course, just as prone to making mistakes as we are, but the information reported is as accurate as we could make it from the records studied, and should provide the researcher with a good beginning point.

We recognize that it is virtually impossible to report such an extensive amount of data without an error creeping in some place. Occasionally, we may have reported a date of birth, which is in reality the date of christening, or vice versa. Many of the dates of birth were taken from the first census record in which the individual appeared, and subsequent records rather often show variations in those dates. Many reported dates of marriage are probably the date a license was issued, as reported in the public records, but should be reasonably close. In some cases, we will report dates as approximate, but they should lead you to the general time frame, so that you may distinguish between individuals with the same name. Throughout the text, I have used terms which should caution the reader: such as, apparently; may have been; reportedly;

about; possibly; could be; and similar terminology, to indicate that the information given has either not been verified by extant contemporary records, or appears to fit a given set of circumstances which, of themselves, are believed to be correct.

Our goal has been to gather all of the available material into one convenient package, which should be accurate enough to provide the casual reader with an insight into their family history. The serious researcher should verify the material with independent research. Good luck, and please forgive our occasional error.

## A WORD OF APPRECIATION

As mentioned in the Introduction, this is the thirty-ninth volume in our series titled generally *Our Maryland Heritage.* None of the books in the series could have been produced without assistance from a number of people; too many to list here individually.

Most importantly, I want to thank Jane Sween, former and now retired librarian of the Montgomery County Historical Society, and the volunteers who worked with her. Beginning with the first volume in the series, Jane had untiringly assisted me with research of the files of the library, with the knowledge that only she possessed. It was also Jane who had guided me toward each new family for study, suggesting which might be the most important for the next effort. She was unquestionably the most valuable resource that could be found in the library, and without her, much of the available information would have been difficult, if not impossible, to find. With her retirement last year, the library was named in her honor, a well-deserved recognition, and we shall miss her presence.

Much encouragement and guidance has since been given me by Pat Anderson, who was for a time Jane's assistant, and is now ably serving as librarian, and by other volunteers at the Historical Society Library. Pat has been a long-time worker at the library, and as a noted genealogist in her own right, will continue to assist all of us in our research. With her knowledge of the resources available, the transition from Jane's retirement has been smooth, without interruption in the valuable services offered by the library. Pat has very quickly become my friend and mentor.

As a result of their continued assistance, from the outset the commitment was made that with publication of each of the books in the series, all royalties derived will continue to be paid directly to the account of the Montgomery County Historical Society, for use of the library.

For we are but little more than single grains in the
sands of time, unless we can determine the common
source from which the total was derived.

- W. N. Hurley, Jr.

CONTENTS

***Order of Presentation***
***Arrangement of the Principal Chapters***

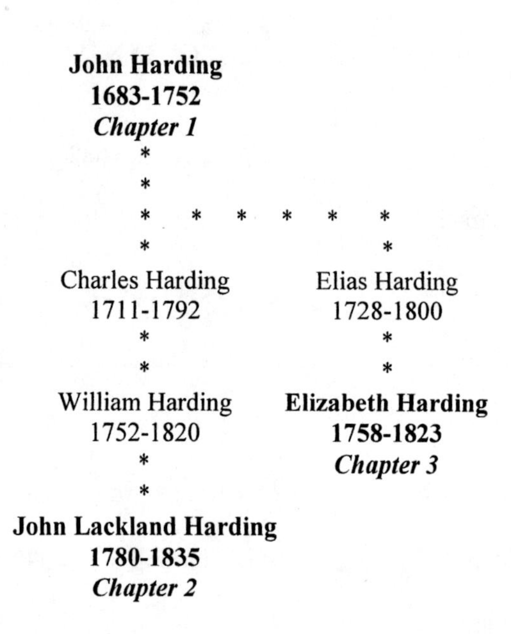


**John W. Harding**
**1789-1861**
***Chapter 4***

Asbury Harding
1814-?

**Zachariah Harding**
**1839-1911**
***Chapter 6***

**Elizabeth Harding**
**1824-1892**
***Chapter 5***

**Elias Harding**
**Died 1832**
***Chapter 7***

**Robert Henry Harding**
**1825-?**
***Chapter 8***

# CHAPTER 1

## John Harding
## 1683-1752

John Harding was born March 25, 1683 in Prince George's County, Maryland and died January 20, 1752 in what was then part of Frederick County, but became Montgomery with its formation in 1776. John is buried in Rockville cemetery on Old Baltimore Road, and his tombstone is said to be the oldest one found in that cemetery. According to the cemetery card files at the Historical Society library, the stone was broken off and repaired, and has carved upon it an hourglass, and a skull and cross-bones.

As early as 1710, John Harding pledged tobacco to the building of a chapel at Rock Creek. Records indicate that his wife was Elizabeth, but her surname is not now known, nor does she appear to be buried with her husband. It has been reported that she was Elizabeth Williams. They are known to have had several children, some of whom were baptized at Saint Barnabas Episcopal Church at Leeland, Queen Anne's Parish.

John left a will in Frederick County, dated January 11, 1751, probated February 5, 1752, recorded in Book A-1 at page 74. To his wife Elizabeth, named as his Executrix, he left the land called *Harding's Choice*, containing one hundred acres, in lieu of her customary one-third of the estate. To his sons Charles and Elias, he left part of the tract called *The Hermitage*, containing 117 acres, to be divided equally between them. Sons Edward and Grove received five shillings each. He provided that three slaves; Coger, Sal and Judsy; be sold and the proceeds be divided between his children: Charles, Lewis, Elizabeth, Lucy, Cassia and Ursely; with the remainder of the estate to his wife.

Elizabeth Harding left a will in Frederick County dated May 31, 1768, probated October 5, 1769, recorded in liber A-1 at page 348. She is clearly the widow of John Harding, naming her children as including Edward, George, Charles, Elias, and Usly (sic), wife of Nathan Holland. She also named several grandchildren: Gary Harding, son of John, to receive forty shillings; the four children of Robert Owen and daughter Keziah Owen to receive one sixth of the estate (without providing their names); sons and daughter of Robert Lazenberry and daughter Lucy to receive one sixth; sons and daughters of Alexander Beall and daughter Elizabeth Beall to receive one sixth. On December 14, 1773, Elias Harding, as Executor of Elizabeth's estate, filed an accounting in liber B-2 at page 298, of Administration Books, listing the estate at 109 pounds, 19 shillings, 10 pence; which included a value of sixty pounds for negro Sam as a gift to Charles Harding.

On June 5, 1719, John Harding purchased 110 acres called *Harding's Choice* from William Beall. It was described as being located on the north side of the northwest branch of the Eastern Branch of the Potomac, at the mouth of a small run a little above the falls of the said branch; and is the same property that John Harding left to his wife Elizabeth in his will.

We also found the will of William Beall, dated January 18, 1756 in Frederick County. He names among his heirs his daughter Elizabeth Harding. Noting the close connections between the Beall and Harding families, we suggest that the wife of John Harding of 1683 was probably Elizabeth Beall, daughter of William Beall and his wife Elizabeth. The children included:

1. Charles Harding, baptized November 26, 1711. He served as a corporal during 1748 in the Troop of Horse under Captain George Beall. He appears to be the same Charles Harding who lived in the Rock Creek Hundred in 1777, and took the Oath of Allegiance February 28, 1778. He was married to Eleanor Davis, daughter of William Davis, Sr. (1694). Charles left a will in Montgomery County dated February 12, 1790, and probated February 14, 1792, recorded in liber B, folio 448. He names Eleanor, and eleven children, not necessarily listed here in birth order:
    a. William Harding, born July 30, 1752, died February 4, 1820. Married to Mary Bell Lackland, who died in May, 1783 in Montgomery County, and was a daughter of John Lackland and Margery Edmonston. John Lackland left a will in Charlotte County, Virginia probated November 6, 1780, in which he names his daughter and her children, confirming the family relationships. William Harding moved his family to Russellville, Kentucky, where he died and is reportedly buried. He had acquired

a tract of about 672 acres of land on the waters of Little Whipperwill Creek in that area, which was the subject of family litigation after his death. Four children:

(1) Margery Harding.

(2) Ellen Harding, predeceased her father. Married to her cousin Elias Harding, son of Walter Harding, and had children, which see under her husband's name.

(3) Anna Harding.

(4) John Lackland Harding, born May 3, 1780, and of whom more in Chapter 2.

b. Clement Harding; took the Oath of Allegiance February 28, 1778 before the Honorable Joseph Wilson.

c. John Harding.

d. Elias Harding.

e. Vachel Harding, baptized February 7, 1763. *Revolutionary Patriots of Montgomery County Maryland 1776-1783*, by Henry C. Peden, Jr. confirms that Vachel was a son of Charles Harding and Eleanor. He applied for a pension on April 5, 1834 in Jefferson County, Kentucky, stating he was then 76 years old. On July 9, 1850, his widow Mary filed for pension at Louisville, Kentucky, based on his Revolutionary War service. She stated that she was formerly Mary Parker, was then 68 years old, and that she had married Vachel Harding March 18, 1798 in Frederick County, Maryland. He died May 11, 1837 in Jefferson County, Kentucky, having been born c.1762, and served as a private in the 5th Co., Lower Battalion, Militia, during 1780. The pension applications indicate that there were children, but they were not named.

f. Benjamin Harding, born or baptized January 23, 1765

g. Lewis Harding.

h. Rezin Harding.

i. Charles Harding.

j. Millicent Harding.

k. Zoeaster Harding.

2. Elizabeth Harding, baptized October 28, 1713, died c.1756; married to Captain Alexander Beall, born c.1712. The Beall Families are treated in extensive detail in *Early Families of*

*Southern Maryland*, Volume 6, by Elsie Greenup Jourdan, 1998, Family Line Publications in Westminster, Maryland. We have not attempted to duplicate nor verify all of that information, and refer the Beall researcher to that work. As the designation Volume 6 suggests, it is one of a series of books on southern Maryland families, and is a valued addition to my own personal library. For our purposes, we will present a brief outline of the descendants of Elizabeth Harding and her husband. Alexander was married again after her death, to Sarah Winters of New Castle County, Delaware, who was the widow of Joseph Ogle, one of the richest men in Frederick County. In 1743, Alexander Beall patented a 200 acre tract called *Jovial Ramble*, then located in Prince George's County (but later in Frederick). In 1756, he was taxed for 91 acres of *Jovial Ramble*; 286 acres of *Discovery*; 50 acres of Jacob's *Cowpen*; 84 acres of *Rubbish*; 84 acres of *Refuse*; 246 ½ acres of *King Cole*; and 259 ½ acres of *The Forrest*. He left a will in Frederick County, dated April 9, 1759, probated May 5, 1759, naming his wife and children, and several of the tracts of land just mentioned. Alexander Beall and Elizabeth Harding were the parents of several children:

a. Leonard Beall, born c.1736, died c.1804 Clark County, Kentucky. Married before August 25, 1763 to Eleanor Magruder, daughter of Zachariah Magruder. They had at least one son:
    (1) Zachariah Harding Beall, born c.1761 in Montgomery County, Maryland, died September, 1826 in old Morgan County, Illinois (now Scott County). Married in Clark County, Kentucky May 15, 1794 to Nancy Ann Evans, born c.1763.
b. William Magruder Beall, died c.1759. Under his father's will, he inherited the tract of land called *King Cole*, with the provision that should he die, it would revert to his sisters Sabrina, Mary and Martha. On February 14, 1769, the three and their spouses filed for a division of the land in accordance with their father's will (Frederick County Deed Book WR-2, folio 61).
c. Elizabeth Beall.

d. Sarah Beall, married to Lawrence Owen, son of Edward Owen.
e. Edward Beall, born October 25, 1743, died December, 1797. Married in Frederick County February 25, 1770 to Rachel Edmonston, born c.1746, daughter of James Edmonston and Mary Beall; and a descendant of Ninian Beall, the immigrant. At least six children.
f. Sabrina Beall, married her cousin, Jeremiah Beall, and had several children.
g. Mary Beall, married Thomas Edmonston, born c.1740, son of Archibald Edmonston and Dorothy Brooke. They had eight children, at least three of whom married into the old Waters family of Montgomery County. See *Our Maryland Heritage, Book Thirty-two, The Waters Families*, 2002, Heritage Books, Bowie, Maryland.
h. Martha Beall.

3. Mary Harding, baptized September 8, 1715.
4. John Harding, baptized April 29, 1718. Married and had at least one son:
   a. Gary Harding.
5. Edward Solluck Harding, baptized June 20, 1720
6. Lewis Harding, baptized April 20, 1722
7. Lucy Harding, baptized October 14, 1724; married to Robert Lazenby, Jr., born c.1725, died c.1785. He was reportedly in the colonial militia of Prince George's County in 1748, the year Frederick County was formed. Robert left a will in Montgomery County, dated March 3, 1785, probated June 14, 1785, recorded in liber B at folio 209, rerecorded in book VMB 1 at page 174. He names his wife as Martha, to whom he left the dwelling house, apparently a second marriage after the death of Lucy. There were also nine children listed there by name. He lived near the present-day area of Montgomery County known as Layhill on the plantation known as *Wolf's Den*, and they had children:
   a. Robert Lazenby, III, born March 27, 1750, died January 13, 1835, perhaps in Virginia. Married Margery Ridgeway, and had at least one son:
      (1) Joshua Lazenby, born September 11, 1775, died January 13, 1867 in Virginia. Married to Ruth

Guthrie, born March 5, 1781, died February 13, 1868, and had at least one son:

(a) John C. Lazenby, born March 30, 1808

b. Henry Lazenby, born c.1760, died c.1835 in Lincoln County, Tennessee. Married to Eleanor Baggerly, born March 20, 1763, and moved to Iredell County, North Carolina. About 1816 he moved with most of his family to Lincoln County, Tennessee. With his brother Alexander, he was a member of the Flying Camp in Maryland, recruited July, 1776. He later served in the 29th Regiment, Lower Battalion with his brothers Alexander, Joshua and Elias.

c. Alexander Lazenby.

d. Joshua Lazenby, born c.1775 according to the 1776 census of the Frederick Hundred.

e. Elias Lazenby, died April 19, 1816 in Georgia, where he had married Martha Jones.

f. Ann Lazenby, born c.1749; married Josiah Jones (1754). At least one daughter:

(1) Margaret Jones, born February 21, 1778, died December 25, 1821. Married as his second wife to Edward Harding, and had at least one child.

g. Elizabeth Lazenby, born February 12, 1763; married Fairall.

h. John Lazenby.

i. Thomas Lazenby.

8. George Harding, baptized October 14, 1724

9. Elias Harding, baptized July 4, 1728, died c.1800. Elias served in the Revolution as Captain, 2nd Co., 29th Battalion from May 14, 1776 to about August 11, 1779. He lived in the Rock Creek Hundred, and in addition to service, also provided wheat for use of the military, and took the Oath of Allegiance before Edward Burgess February 28, 1778. This Elias Harding left a will in Montgomery County dated November 10, 1799, probated March 10, 1800, recorded in liber D at folio 295; and rerecorded in book VMB 1 at page 439. He named his wife Elizabeth, and left specific bequests to a number of children and grandchildren, most of them by name. He was married to Elizabeth Beall, born c.1719, one of the

daughters of William Beall, Sr. and Jane Edmonston of Frederick County. (Some records indicate that her parents were William Beall and Elizabeth Magruder, which has not been confirmed.) The children were:

a. Edward Harding; received the negro boy named Enos. He served during the Revolution as a private in the 2nd and the 5th companies of the Lower Battalion, Militia, under Captain Edward Burgess. Edward was married May 12, 1779 to Ann Butler, reportedly his first marriage. They had at least two sons and a daughter. Ann Butler was a daughter of Thomas Butler, who served in the Revolution, and had arrived in America with the Carroll family, and owned about nine thousand acres of land in the Montgomery County area. Edward was married second May 21, 1814 to Margaret Jones, born February 21, 1778, died December 25, 1821, the daughter of Josiah Jones (1754) and Ann Lazenby (1749). She was first married January 24, 1799 to James Wilson Perry, who died October 30, 1809, and by whom she had children. Edward Harding and his second wife also had one child. The known children were:
   (1) Henry Harding, born c.1782, of whom more.
   (2) Caroline Frances Harding, born c.1793, of whom more.
   (3) Edward Harding, Jr., served for many years as a major in the army.
   (4) Josiah Harding, born c.1817, of whom more.
b. Josiah Harding, born c.1764, received the negro named Ben. He served as a private in the 2nd Co., under Captain Edward Burgess, Lower District, Militia, during July, 1776, and took the Oath of Allegiance February 28, 1778. Josiah died about 1820, apparently in Kentucky.
c. Nathan Harding, received the negro named Davy, and all the remainder of the tract called *Forrest* after the bequest to his brother John. Nathan married Rebecca and died c.1803 in Brooke County, West Virginia, according to a report found in the family folder file at the Historical Society library in Rockville. However, the library also contains records of St. Peter's Church at Poolesville, in

which a daughter of Nathan and Rebecca is reported, the dates appearing to conflict with the reported move to West Virginia. It should also be noted that West Virginia did not exist in 1803 when Nathan reportedly died there. We have also found a report that Nathan had at least one son as well:

(1) Josiah Harding, born c.1790

(2) Elizabeth Harding, born January 21, 1799, died September 29, 1826.

d. John Harding, received the negro named Ezekiel. At the death of his mother, he was to receive one hundred and fifty acres adjacent to the tract called *Forrest* upon which his father then lived. He served as a private in the 2nd Co., under Captain Edward Burgess, Lower District, Militia, during July, 1776, as well as private in the 6th Co., and took the Oath of Allegiance on February 28, 1778. Married and had children, only one of them named in his father's will, but provision made that should that one grandson be deceased, the bequest would be divided between his brothers and sisters. Only known child is:

(1) Thomas Noble Harwood Harding, received one negro boy named Scipio from his grandfather's will.

e. Walter Harding, who predeceased his father, leaving children named in the father's will. Walter left a will in Montgomery County dated May 6, 1782, probated August 16, 1782, recorded in liber B at folio 88; rerecorded in book VMB 1, page 119. He named his widow Mary, and five children, leaving everything to his wife so long as she remained his widow, and not remarried. In the event of her remarriage, she was to receive one third, with the other two thirds being divided equally between the five children. She was apparently Mary Murphy, a daughter of Philip Murphy, and was married second about 1783 to Samuel Sprigg and had one child (Rebecca Sprigg, born September 19, 1790). There is reportedly an inventory of the estate of Walter Harding, dated October 16, 1787, by Samuel Sprigg (liber B, folio 351), for the benefit of the orphans of Walter Harding. It reports that Elias Harding was then in Lexington

County, Kentucky; that his daughter Polly was married to Drane; and his son Philip was married to Amelia and then lived in Elkton. The children were:

(1) Margery Harding, born October 11, 1774, perhaps died in childhood.
(2) Elias Harding, died c.1838, and of whom more.
(3) Philip Harding, born September 19, 1780; married Amelia and had children:
    (a) Mary Elizabeth Harding.
    (b) Walter Harding.
    (c) Amelia Ann Harding.
    (d) Philip Thomas Harding.
(4) Mary Harding, born January 15, 1778; married to Thomas O. Drane, and lived in Kentucky. In his letter of 1820 to his mother, Elias Harding reported that "Mr. Drane is getting rich."
(5) Elizabeth Harding, married to Benjamin Williams.
(6) Anna Harding; named in her father's will, but not in the will of her grandfather.

f. Basil Harding, predeceased his father, leaving children named in the will of his father. He served as a private in the 2nd Co., Lower District, Militia, during September, 1777, and as a corporal in the 5th Co. during July 15, 1780, and took the Oath of Allegiance February 28, 1778 before the Honorable Edward Burgess. Reportedly married to Ann Hooper Wheeler and had children:
   (1) Mary Harding.
   (2) Sarah Harding.
   (3) Elizabeth Harding.
   (4) Walter Harding.

g. Elizabeth Harding, born c.1758, died September 1, 1823, and of whom more in Chapter 3.

h. Deborah Harding, born c.1769 in an area of Frederick County, Maryland which became part of Montgomery County when it was formed in 1776. She reportedly died about December, 1836, probably in Kentucky. She was married February 25, 1785, presumably in Montgomery County, Maryland, to John Hanson Wheeler, said to have been born about 1757 in Dorchester County, Maryland, son of John Wheeler. They had a number of children, all apparently born in Montgomery County prior to a family move to Kentucky:

(1) Elizabeth Wheeler, born December 7, 1786, died April 13, 1813. Married January 2, 1802 in what later became Brooke County, West Virginia to Charles Miller.

(2) Mary Hooper Wheeler, born March 22, 1788, died December 15, 1822. Married January 19, 1810 in what became West Virginia to Joseph Rose.

(3) Mahala Wheeler, born August 15, 1789, died July 18, 1849. Married March 31, 1818 in Jefferson County, Kentucky to Ulysses Rose.

(4) Ann Hooper Wheeler, born April 21, 1791, died April 10, 1855, probably in an area that became West Virginia. Married January 28, 1813 to William Chapline.

(5) John Hanson Wheeler, Jr., born February 10, 1793, died December 5, 1867. Married April 27, 1826 in Oldham County, Kentucky to Susan Penn Payne.

(6) Josiah Harding Wheeler, born December 12, 1795, died February 12, 1837 at Simpsonville, Kentucky. Married January 13, 1820 in Kentucky to Malvina Adelaide Russell.

(7) Sarah Wheeler, born January 6, 1797, died January 11, 1862. Married January 13, 1820 in Kentucky to Joshua G. Barclay.

(8) Elias Harding Wheeler, born October 8, 1798, died May 8, 1857, probably Trimble County, Kentucky.

(9) Emily Wheeler, born April 27, 1800, died January 22, 1823 in Oldham County, Kentucky. Married April 4, 1820 in Jefferson County, Kentucky to Milton Wilson.

(10) Matilda Perry Wheeler, born October 24, 1801, died October 13, 1821 in Kentucky. Married there February 26, 1820 to George W. Barclay.

(11) Henrietta W. Wheeler, born March 31, 1803, died September 9, 1821 in Kentucky. Married there March 8, 1821 to Joseph H. Ashbridge.

(12) Priscilla Wheeler, born January 28, 1805, died May 27, 1850. Married October 2, 1828 to Adam Kuhn.
(13) Albert Perry Wheeler, born February 14, 1808 in an area that later became West Virginia, died July 28, 1863. Married there June 4, 1832 to Ophelia Duval.
(14) Truman White Wheeler, born December 20, 1808, died September 22, 1827.
(15) Ulysses Hanson Wheeler, born August 14, 1811, died August 14, 1827

10. Grove Harding, baptized September 1, 1729
11. Cassia Harding. This is perhaps the same as Keziah Harding, married to Robert Owen. Cassia appeared in the will of her father, and as Keziah in the will of her mother. In the will of her mother, reference is made to the four children of this couple, but does not name them. Robert left a will in Montgomery County, dated May 11, 1779, probated July 4, 1779, recorded in liber A at folio 175, rerecorded in book VMB 1 at page 53. He named a wife Mary, suggesting a second marriage, and eight children, at least four of whom were born to Cassia or Keziah Harding. To the first three listed sons, he left the lands located on Rock Creek, and to son Washington Owen, he left the home plantation. The tract called *Shepherd's Hard Fortune*, where the testator's father had lived, was to be sold. The three boys were all said to be under twenty-one years of age, and the girls were all minors. It appears likely that only the first four were children of Keziah. In the order they appeared in the will, the children were:
    a. Edward Owen, born November 23, 1763
    b. Robert Owen.
    c. Washington Owen.
    d. Eleanor Owen.
    e. Ann Owen.
    f. Elizabeth Owen.
    g. Mary Owen.
    h. Octavia Owen, married June 5, 1802 to Eli Beall in Montgomery County.
12. Ursely Harding, perhaps Ursula. Married Nathan Holland.

## Henry Harding
## 1782-1863

This son of Edward Harding and Ann Butler was born c.1782 in Montgomery County, Maryland, and buried in June, 1863 at St. Mary's old cemetery in Rockville. Head of household in the 1850 census of the Rockville District of Montgomery County, Henry was listed with $6,800 in real estate and was then serving as Register of Wills for the county. At the time of the 1850 census, Henry Harding was the owner of four slaves. He was married in the county by license dated June 2, 1812 to Catherine Ann Robb, born c.1792, listed with her husband. Living with them was Ellen R. Queen, born c.1834, and apparently three children. Head of household in the 1860 census of the Fourth District, Henry was listed owning $15,500 in real estate and $9,700 in personal property. His wife Catharine was still present, with the same children. She left a will in Montgomery County, dated December 22, 1857, probated September 29, 1863, recorded in liber JWS 1 at folio 148. Her heirs were specified as her two daughters. Children were:

1. Mary Anna Harding, born October 29, 1815; baptized November 9, 1815 at eleven days old (records of St. John's Catholic Church at Forest Glen. Her *Sentinel* obituary of January 25, 1907 states that she died January 6, 1907 at the home of her son-in-law John Maurie Dove of Washington. She was the mother of eight children, seven of whom predeceased her. Married in Montgomery County by license dated November 19, 1839 to Robert W. Carter, who served as Register of Wills for many years in Montgomery County. His obituary in the *Sentinel* stated that he was born September 2, 1812 in Prince George's County, and died August 12, 1890 at his home in Rockville. He moved to Montgomery County as a boy to be educated, living with his half-brother, John A. Carter. He later went to Arkansas for a time, but returned to Rockville, and about 1870 was elected Register of Wills. The obituary states that of his six sons and two daughters, only two were living at the time of his death; Henry H. Carter and Mrs. Maury Dove. He was buried at St. Mary's Cemetery in Rockville. Robert was head of household in the 1850 census of the Fourth District of the county, listed next door to the

family of his father-in-law, Henry Harding (1782). Robert was a lawyer, owning $6,000 in real estate. His wife Mary A. was present, and they then had five children. He was next found as head of household in the 1860 census of the Fourth District, for the Rockville Post Office, born c.1813, listed as a lawyer, owning $7,000 in real estate and $8,000 in personal property. His wife was listed there as Mary A., and they then had six children at home. Robert W. Carter was next found as head of household in the 1870 census of the Fourth District, now reported as Register of Wills, owning $11,000 in real estate and $2,000 in personal property. His wife Mary A. was there, with six children still at home. Listed simply as Robert Carter, Register of Wills, he was head of household in the 1880 census of the Fourth District, with his wife Mary, and two of the children still at home; John and Annie. Children:

a. Henry Harding Carter, September 10, 1840, a clerk. At home in 1860, reported as a civil engineer. His *Sentinel* obituary reports that he died December 28, 1895, leaving a widow. He was married in Prince George's County, October 15, 1873 to Mary Moylan Gunton. She died July 6, 1897 at home in Washington. (*Sentinel* obituary).
b. Robert W. Carter, Jr., born July 8, 1844; not at home in 1860. Reportedly died in Ohio of pneumonia during the Civil War; apparently single.
c. Charles Adam Carter, born October 10, 1846, died March 17, 1880 at Rockville of typhoid fever. In the 1860 census of the Fourth District, Charles was living in the household of Horatio James (1796), a miller, two dwellings removed from that of his parents. In 1870, he was again found in the family listings with his parents and siblings. Apparently single.
d. John Alexander Carter, a twin, born December 26, 1848, died March 10, 1890 at his father's home in Rockville.
e. James Caldwell Carter, a twin, born December 26, 1848. In the 1870 census, he was listed as deputy register, apparently serving with his father. The *Sentinel* of March 30, 1877 reported that he died "recently."
f. Catherine Carter, born August 29, 1851, died February 8, 1856

g. William Carter, born November 26, 1853, died September 1, 1874 at his parents home near Rockville.
h. Elizabeth Ann Carter, born July 18, 1856, died November 19, 1929 in Washington; buried at Rock Creek Cemetery. Married in the county by license dated September 5, 1882 to John Maury Dove. The *Sentinel* reported the wedding of that date, listing her name as Miss Nannie Carter. The 1870 census of the Fourth District reported a daughter of the proper age as Nannie Carter, apparently the same individual. At least one son:
   (1) William T. Dove, an infant death July 22, 1891

2. Elizabeth Ann Harding, born July 4, 1815, baptized September 14, 1815, died January 14, 1862, single. Records of St. John's Catholic Church at Forest Glen. We note that the date of birth conflicts with that of her sister Mary Ann Harding, reported just above, with only three months difference.
3. Charles Adam Harding, born September 28, 1820, died June 1, 1892, a physician; buried at St. Mary's cemetery, Rockville. Sponsor to his baptism was Caroline Frances (Harding) Noland, married in the county by license dated January 11, 1816 to Dade Noland. She was an aunt of Charles, sister of his father. At the time of the 1850 census, Charles A. Harding owned nine slaves. He went south and enlisted as a private, Company C, 2nd Maryland Cavalry, CSA, and fought throughout the War Between The States, and later settled in Prince George's County, Maryland. In the family folder file at the Historical Society library, there was a print of the will of Charles Adam Harding, which is apparently this individual. It is not referenced, but was dated July 14, 1847. His mother Catherine was to receive his entire estate for her life, and after that to be divided equally between his sisters, not named. Charles was married, however, to Vidie Lee, and the will may have been voided.
4. William R. Harding, baptized August 23, 1818; records of St. John's Catholic Church at Forest Glen. Killed on the streets of Augusta, Georgia.
5. Catharine Jane Harding, born October 23, 1824, died June 26, 1897. Married October 2, 1866 as his second wife to Doctor Charles J. Maddox, born December 31, 1819, buried in St.

Mary's Catholic Church cemetery in Rockville. He was a son of William Theobald Maddox (1790) and Anna Maria King (1800). He was first married October 7, 1851 to Mary Lemmon King (1830) of Georgetown, by whom he had several children. No children were born to Catharine Jane Harding, although she assumed the role of mother to the children of her husband during the thirty years of their marriage. Catherine's father Henry Harding was a man of prominence; for a time he was the county sheriff and afterward became a member of the state Legislature; and still later served as Register of Wills. His wife was a daughter of Adam Robb, who was born in Scotland and emigrated to America in his youth. By division of the estate of Adam Robb, Catharine Jane Harding Maddox, his granddaughter, was allocated a tract of 156 and 1/2 acres of land at Rockville, known as *McGrath Place*, on which she and her husband, Dr. Charles John Maddox resided when they moved into Rockville. Her will, dated August 8, 1883 and probated in Montgomery County, Maryland July 13, 1897 is found in Liber GCD 2 at folio 460. It is a very simple will, leaving her property in trust to Samuel Jones, who is to administer and invest the estate, with the proceeds thereof to go to her husband, Doctor Charles J. Maddox for his maintenance and support. At his death, her estate is to be divided between the children of her husband. The descendants of Doctor Maddox are set forth in extensive detail in our earlier book, *Maddox, A Southern Maryland Family*, published 1994 by Heritage Books, Inc.

**Caroline Frances Harding**
**1793-**

This daughter of Edward Harding and Ann Butler was born c.1793, died c.1863. She was listed as sponsor at the birth of Charles Adam Harding in 1820, one of the sons of Henry Harding (1782), just above, suggesting a family relationship. She was married in the county by license dated January 11, 1816 to Dade P. Noland, born c.1780 and reared on a farm in Virginia.

Dade was the descendant of an Irish immigrant, and had served in the War of 1812, following in the footsteps of his father

Thomas Noland, who served in the Revolution. Thomas Noland left a will in Loudoun County, Virginia, dated February 2, 1811, in which he named his wife as Eleanor, and left a negro man Samuel to his son Dade Noland. Also to Dade, jointly with his brothers Samuel and Lloyd, their father left the lands located in Loudoun County. The will makes it clear that Thomas Noland also owned land in Frederick County, Maryland, and had several sons and daughters, including Dade.

At the time of his marriage, Dade Noland lived at Noland's Ferry near Leesburg, Virginia, and was engaged in merchandising in Virginia, and remained there for a short period thereafter. Some time after their wedding, he moved to Montgomery County, where he engaged in farming until his death in 1838. Witnesses at her wedding included Edward Harding, Sr. (her father), Edward Harding, Jr. (her brother); Henry Harding of 1782 (her brother), and other members of the family.

Widowed in 1838, Caroline F. Noland was found as head of household in the 1850 census of the Fifth District, born c.1793, with $2,000 in real estate, and seventeen slaves, and with four children at home. She then owned 200 acres of improved land and 50 acres of unimproved land, 7 horses, 8 milch cows, 2 working oxen, 1 other cattle, 40 sheep and 17 swine. In the previous year, she had produced 200 bushels of wheat, 25 bushels of rye, 500 bushels of Indian corn, 200 bushels of oats, 120 pounds of wool, 80 bushels of Irish potatoes, 300 pounds of butter, and 15 tons of hay. With 200 acres in production, and seventeen slaves, she was operating a working farm. No other member of the Noland family was reported in the 1850 census of the county. Caroline was next found as head of household in the 1860 census of the Fifth District, for the Sandy Spring Post Office area, with the four children still at home (although we transcribed the surname as Nolan). She then was listed as owning $8,000 in real estate and $16,265 in personal property, in large measure probably the value of slaves. In the 1867-1868 Slave Census of Montgomery County, Agnes Noland, as Administrator, listed thirty-four slaves (by name and age) owned by the heirs of Caroline F. Noland. The children were:

1. Jane Elizabeth Noland, born c.1822; baptized August 25, 1822 at one month of age; records of St. John's Catholic Church at Forest Glen. She died December 31, 1892 at her

home near Rockville; buried at St. Mary's Cemetery, adjacent to the church in Rockville. Married February 21, 1843 to Joseph T. Bailey. His obituary in the *Sentinel* stated that he died on November 16, 1881 at his home near Rockville, in his $72^{nd}$ year. He had served on the Board of the County Commissioners in 1865 and 1879, and was the father of thirteen years, all of them surviving their father. Born c.1807 in New York, he was head of household in the 1850 census of the Fourth District of Montgomery County, owning $5,000 in real estate. His wife Jane was listed, with four children. He was next found as head of household in the 1860 census of the Fourth District, with his wife Jane, and ten children. He then was listed with $10,000 in real estate and $1,500 in personal property. He was also head of household in the 1870 census of the Fourth District, with $8,000 in real estate and $1,000 in personal property. His wife Jane and eight children were at home. In the 1880 census of the Fourth District, Joseph T. and Jane were found with five of their children still at home. The children were:

a. Mary C. Bailey, born c.1844; not at home in 1870
b. Joseph T. Bailey, Jr., born c.1845; perhaps married in the county by license dated May 2, 1871 to Attelia Clagett.
c. James D. Bailey, born c.1848; not at home in 1870
d. Lewis Bailey, born c.1849; not at home in 1870. His obituary in the *Sentinel* of January 29, 1886 states that he died "recently" in Arizona where he had been living since 1868. Only his mother was mentioned.
e. Edward Bailey, born c.1852. Perhaps this individual, the *Sentinel* of May 10, 1878 reported that Edward Bailey of Rockville left Monday to visit his brothers in Baltimore, New Jersey, New York and Arizona, after which he would move to Kansas where he planned to farm.
f. Agnes Bailey, born c.1854
g. Celesta Bailey, born c.1855; read as Calista in 1870. In the 1880 census, there is a daughter reported as Anna, one year older than Thomas (next), who may be this child; the name Anna not having occurred earlier.

h. Thomas Bailey, born c.1856; in the 1880 census reported as born c.1860, which does not appear correct. He was head of household in the 1900 census of the Fourth District, a widower, born July, 1857. Living with him was his sister Agnes (above), single, and two children:
   (1) Thomas E. Bailey, born November, 1895
   (2) Irene Bailey, born May, 1898
i. Irene Bailey, born c.1850. We question the date of birth, in that the children were listed in the 1860 census in the order here reported, suggesting that Irene should have been no more than three years of age, although reported from the census as ten years. Further, all the children between the ages of five and fifteen were noted as being in school, but not Irene. Not listed in 1870. Perhaps the same Irene Bailey married in the county by license dated November 5, 1867 to Thomas W. Entwhistle. They were not found in a later census.
j. Stephen Bailey, born c.1859; not at home in 1870. The Sentinel of April 4, 1879 reported that Stephen left his home the previous Friday to live in Urbana, Ohio.
k. John D. Bailey, born c.1862; at home in 1880
l. William Bailey, born c.1863; at home in 1880
m. Jane Bailey, born c.1865; at home in 1880

2. Ann Butler Noland, baptized February 16, 1824 at eight days of age; records of St. John's Catholic Church at Forest Glen.
3. Thomas Edward Noland, born c.1826 in the Berry District, Montgomery County, died August 26, 1898 at his home near Wheaton survived by two brothers and two sisters. Records of St. John's Catholic Church at Forest Glen report his baptism on October 16, 1826 at four weeks of age. Married in 1867 to Maria Pearce, who died August 2, 1885, daughter of William C. Pearce. Thomas was head of household in the 1870 census of the Fifth District, with his wife, Maria, born c.1832, but no children. The *Sentinel* reported that she died August 2, 1885 at the age of fifty-four, in the Berry District of the county. In the 1880 census of the Fifth District the couple again appeared, without children. He was a slave-owner prior to the war, and served as a judge of elections, and in 1876 as clerk of the house of representatives.

4. Agnes M. Noland, born January 26, 1828, died May 27, 1915, single; buried at St. John's Catholic Church at Forest Glen. In the 1880 census of the Fourth District, Agnes was single, operating a boarding house, with her brother James living there, also single. There were also three boarders, and one black servant to complete the listing. The age for Agnes was correct at 52 years, but James was reported at only 45 years, about four too young.
5. Sylvester Noland, baptized June 24, 1829 at seven weeks old; records of St. John's Catholic Church at Forest Glen.
6. James C. Noland, born March c.1831, died March 26, 1901. In the 1870 census of the Fifth District, James was found as head of household, with his sister Agnes living with him. They were listed next door to the household of their brother Thomas Noland. In the 1900 census of the Thirteenth District, James was head of household, listed as a retired farmer, single. Living with him was his sister Agnes M. Noland, single, keeping house. He was reported there as born March, 1831 and Agnes as January, 1828, both apparently correct.
7. Mary Caroline Noland, born January 30, 1833, died July 7, 1910; buried at St. Mary's old cemetery, Rockville, with her husband. Not listed in 1860 census. Married in the county by license dated September 5, 1868 to Sylvester C. Jones, born September 22, 1832 in the Potomac District, died January 23, 1907, son of John Jones of N (1785) and Catherine Offutt (daughter of Andrew Offutt). They were the parents of eleven children, including Sylvester, who was the last surviving member of that family. The great grandfather of Sylvester Jones was Nathan Jones, an English nobleman, who emigrated to America, becoming a landed proprietor in what is now Montgomery County. Sylvester was head of household in the 1870 census of the Fifth District, born c.1837, owning $5,000 in real estate and $1,000 in personal property. His wife Carrie (diminutive form for Caroline) was there, and they then had one child. Sylvester was next found listed only by his initials, as S. C. Jones, head of household in the 1880 census of the Fourth District, with his wife reported as Carrie M. Noland, with five black servants, and five children living at home. Sylvester was next head of household in the 1900

census of the Potomac District, with his wife now listed as Mary C., her full name perhaps being Mary Caroline. Her father (Dade Noland) was there reported as having been born in Virginia, the first time we have noted that entry. Married for thirty-one years, she had been the mother of six children, only four of them surviving, and two at home. In addition to their natural children, Sylvester C. Jones and Mary Caroline Noland adopted Catherine Vernon, who was married in January, 1924 to John Charles Yates of Washington. The children included:

a. Sylvester Noland Jones, born July 24, 1869; attended Georgetown College for two years, and died July 24, 1889; buried with his parents.

b. John F. Jones, born c.1871; as a young man operated an agricultural implements business in Washington.

c. Mary Caroline Jones, born April 7, 1874, died November 12, 1941; buried at St. Mary's Cemetery in Rockville. Married in the county November 8, 1908 to Elbert Thomas Clagett, born c.1874; son of Henry M. Clagett (1834) and Mary Elizabeth Shaw (1850). Some records report this child as Lena M. Jones, reversing the given names, and using a diminutive form for Caroline, which tends to confuse the records.

d. Theodore Jones, born March 7, 1876 near Rockville, died May 2, 1938 at his home on 10th Street, NW, in Washington. Married to Alena Mannakee, born about September, 1880, daughter of William E. Mannakee (1851) and Carrie Bond. Alena has also been found as Alma, including in the obituary of her husband. Her father was a dealer in grain, flour and feed at Silver Spring, and the operator of Burnt Mills, making fine flours. About 1898 Theodore was engaged in the mercantile business in Philadelphia, but apparently returned to Montgomery County. Married for two years, without children, they were found in the household of her father in the 1900 census of the Fifth District. Children:

   (1) Lucille Jones, married to Hoskinson.

   (2) Eleanor Jones.

e. James Hampton Jones, born November 28, 1877, died January 15, 1965 at his home on West Montgomery Avenue in Rockville; buried at St. Mary's Cemetery in Rockville. Married July 21, 1915 to Ethel May Pate, he was a retired vice president of the Farmers Banking and Trust Company. His wife died February 16, 1978 at Gaithersburg and was buried with her husband. They had children:

(1) James Hampton Jones, Jr., born May 9, 1916, died January 25, 1968. Married September 20, 1947 to Barbara Ramsdell, and lived on Alden Avenue in Gaithersburg; buried at St. Rose Catholic Cemetery near Gaithersburg. At the time of death, he was general manager of the Casey Development Corporation, a post he had held for about thirty years. He served during the second world war as a master sergeant, and was a Fourth Degree member of the Knights of Columbus, among numerous other civic and community activities. During the author's years in the surveying business, Eugene B. Casey was a frequent client, and Hampy Jones became a good and trusted friend. Five children:

(a) Anne Brooks Jones.
(b) Frances Elizabeth Jones.
(c) Charles Eugene Jones.
(d) Mark Hampton Jones.
(e) Andrew Paul Jones.

(2) Stephen Noland Jones, born July 13, 1920; a doctor practicing in Rockville; the author having been among his patients. Married July 23, 1958 in St. Patrick's Cathedral in New York to Ann Crowley, daughter of Vincent Crowley. She had appeared in the London Company of *Oklahoma*, and continued to perform occasionally after their marriage. They had four children:

(a) Kelly Jones, born c.1959
(b) Elisa Jones, born c.1960
(c) Thomas Jones, born c.1963
(d) Blaise Vincent Jones, born July 4, 1965

(3) Mary Virginia Jones, married c.1949 to Emmett G. Murphy and lived in Gaithersburg. He died January 16, 1993, leaving his wife and children:
  (a) Mary Alice Murphy.
  (b) Nancy Murphy, married to Azano.
  (c) Teresa Murphy.
  (d) Patricia Murphy.
  (e) Susan Murphy, married to Mack.

(4) Caroline Elizabeth Jones, married to John Cook and lived in Youngstown, Ohio.

(5) Martha Ann Jones, married to Frank Porfido and lived in Dover, New Jersey.

(6) Charles Eugene Jones, born April 7, 1922, apparently died young.

f. Frederick Thomas Jones, born August 16, 1872; an infant death.

8. Fanny Noland, born c.1838; appeared only in the 1860 census. However, in the *Sentinel* obituary of Thomas E. Noland, it is stated that he was survived by two brothers and two sisters, indicating that the listing we present here is correct.
9. Samuel S. Noland.
10. Mary Ellen Noland, died at the age of sixteen.
11. Anna Butler Noland, died at the age of twenty. We note that *Portrait and Biographical Record of the Sixth Congressional District, Maryland*, by Chapman Publishing Co. states that the children in this family included three sons and five daughters. We here report three sons and six daughters; unless this child and the Fanny reported just above are the same individuals.

## Josiah Harding
## 1817-1894

This son of Edward Harding and his second wife, Margaret Jones (1778), the only child born to that union, was a physician, born c.1817 in Maryland, and died January 6, 1894 at his home near Sligo. His *Sentinel* obituary reported that he was survived by his widow and several children, and that he was a half-brother of the late Henry Harding (1782), and was born and reared in Montgomery County. The mother of Josiah died when he was an infant, and his father when he was only about nine years of age; and he was thereafter raised by his half-brother Henry. In the 1850 census of the Fifth District, he was found living in the household of Ann Carroll, and apparently then had a wife Mary, and one small child. Also living in the same household was Benjamin F. Sands, born c.1813, listed as a naval officer, with a wife and five children. Doctor Josiah Harding was married in Montgomery County by license dated November 17, 1846 to Mary Virginia Valdenar, born c.1826, died May 19, 1912. She was a daughter of Francis Valdenar of Berry District, born c.1797, and his wife Elizabeth Culver, born c.1773, to whom he was married in the county by license dated March 28, 1821. In the 1870 census of the Fifth District, the elderly Valdenar couple are shown with their grandson Francis Harding living with them. Francis Valdenar was a prosperous farmer, then owning $11,000 in real estate and $5,000 in personal property. In the 1867-1868 Slave Census of Montgomery County, he was listed as the owner of thirty-three slaves, all reported there by name and age.

In the 1860 census of the Fifth District for the Cottage Post Office, Doctor Josiah Harding was still living in the household of Ann Carroll, who was apparently quite wealthy, with $280 in real estate, but $10,000 in personal property. Josiah was listed as owning $9,275 in personal property. His wife Mary was present and they then had four children. The family of Benjamin F. Sands was still living in the household, and he was then listed as a Commander in the Navy, with $10,500 in real estate.

Head of household in the 1870 census of the Fifth District of Montgomery County, Doctor Josiah Harding owned $8,000 in real estate and $1,500 in personal property. His wife Mary was listed, with six children, and three black servants listed in the household. Head of household in the 1880 census of the Fifth District of Montgomery County, Doctor Josiah Harding was listed with his wife Mary V. (sic) and two daughters. Living in the household was Francis Valdenar, his father-in-law. Also in the household was Charles E. Carter, born c.1845 in New York, a boarder, and apparently his wife, Emily Carter, born c.1846. There was also Georgia Remington, born c.1845 in Canada, married, listed as a boarder. Mary V. Harding was found as head of household in the

1900 census of the Thirteenth District, born October, 1824 in Maryland, and was a widow. She had been the mother of ten children, with three of them surviving, and two living at home. It appears possible that Mary Virginia (Valdenar) Harding is the same Mary Virginia Harding who left a will in Montgomery County, dated September 9, 1891, which was three years before the death of her husband. The will leaves her entire estate to her daughter Henrietta Maria Harding and, although the Mary Virginia we are here discussing died in 1912, the will was not probated until January 18, 1916 and recorded in liber HCA 19 at folio 65. It is perhaps only a coincidence of names, but appears to be possible that we are dealing with the same individual. The children included:

1. Francis V. Harding, born c.1849, died February 16, 1906. In the 1870 census of the Fifth District, he was found living in the household of his Valdenar grandparents. He later lived and worked for a time in Kentucky, but apparently returned to Maryland, and the family home near Forest Glen. Still living at home in the 1900 census, presumably single.
2. Lucy Harding, born c.1854; not at home in 1870
3. William Harding, born c.1855
4. Mary V. Harding, born c.1858.
5. Marian Sands Harding, a daughter, born c.1861. Married in the county May 26, 1881 to William R. Riley at Grace Episcopal Church, perhaps at Sligo, where her family lived.
6. Kate Harding, born c.1863
7. Lizzie Harding, born c.1865
8. Henrietta W. Harding, born c.1868; lived at home as of 1900 (could she be Henrietta Maria Harding?).

### Elias Harding
### Died 1838

This son of Walter Harding was married three times, and had children. He was first married February 24, 1799 to his cousin Ellen Harding, daughter of William Harding (1752). She died October 20, 1814, and he was married second February 25, 1816 to Lucy Claiborn Dunscomb, born June 20, 1773, died April 17, 1828; and third on February 12, 1831 to Rebecca Kelly. In the family file at the Historical Society library in Rockville, there is a typed copy of a letter Elias wrote to his mother. It is dated September 14, 1820 at Logan County, Kentucky; addressed to Mrs. Mary Sprigg, near Barnesville, Montgomery County, Maryland, indicating that she had remarried after the death of Elias' father. The letter notes that uncle Josiah "is no more" having died about the previous May. "Old Mr. Harding is no more, he departed this life in February last." That would be the father of the first wife of Elias. Four of his children are named in the letter. Children:

1. Roger Harding, born October 20, 1799, died October 24, 1827. In the letter of his father, said to be studying medicine.
2. William L. Harding, born October 6, 1801, died about July 25, 1835. His father's letter of 1820 suggests that he will probably become a lawyer. Married to America Heise by license dated October 20, 1825.
3. Mary Ann Harding, born April 12, 1805, died September 3, 1825; married to Price.
4. Margery Lackland Harding, born March 24, 1807, died May 6, 1855; married December 21, 1826 to Thompson Harding.
5. Margaret Louisa Shepherd Harding, born August 13, 1808, died October 30, 1827
6. George Washington Harding, born c.1810, died December 10, 1827
7. Walter Philip Harding, born August 26, 1812, died September 16, 1856. Married October 27, 1835 to Elizabeth Higgason Rice, born September 3, 1817, died February 22, 1860. They apparently had at least these children:
   a. George Phillip Harding, born January 20, 1842
   b. Elizabeth Ellen Harding, born March 19, 1842
   c. Lucy Rice Harding, born April 8, 1848

# CHAPTER 2

## John Lackland Harding
## 1780-1835

This son of William Harding (1752) and Mary Bell Lackland was born May 3, 1780 in Montgomery County, Maryland. John did not appear to go to Kentucky with his father. John L. served as a private in the War of 1812 in the company of Captain Henry Steiner, in the volunteers from Frederick, discharged at Baltimore in October, 1814. In 1823, John L. ran for mayor of the city of Frederick in which he was successful. In his official capacity, he led the welcoming committee on the occasion of the visit to the city by Marquis de La Fayette with his son, George Washington La Fayette. John L. Harding was later Justice of the Orphan's Court, and Chief Justice between the years 1831 and 1835. He died in Frederick County, Maryland on October 15, 1835, as reported in *The John Engelbrecht Death Ledger of Frederick County, Maryland 1820-1890*, by Edith Olivia Eader and Trudie Davis-Long, 1995. John was married twice, first on May 31, 1804 to Eleanor Marshall, daughter of James Marshall. She died March 31, 1816, and John married secondly March 10, 1820 to Eleanor Mantz, daughter of Francis Mantz of Fredericktown. His second wife died October 2, 1835. He had six children from his first marriage and three from the second:

1. Mary Harding, married in Frederick County July 25, 1830 to Nimrod Bantz. Apparently at least one son:
   a. Arthur Bantz, born c.1844, died April 19, 1865 in St. Genevieve, Missouri.
2. Elizabeth L. Harding, born c.1809, died December 18, 1862; buried at Mt. Olivet Cemetery in Frederick with her husband. Married July 10, 1834 to Lieutenant Joseph Stalling, USN, who died April 25, 1841. Elizabeth was listed as head of household in the 1850 census of Fredericktown, apparently a widow, with three children:
   a. Ellen M. Stalling, born c.1836
   b. Joseph Stalling, born c.1839
   c. Charles L. Stalling, born c.1841

3. Caroline T. Harding, died September 29, 1868 in Baltimore.
4. William Harrison Harding, married April 9, 1831 to Mahala C. Parsons.
5. James Marshall Harding, born August 28, 1808, died January 12, 1873; buried at Mt. Olivet Cemetery in Frederick with his wife. Married December 1, 1840 to Sarah Ann Fleming Hall, who died December 19, 1895; former wife of John H. Hall, to whom she was married February 24, 1831, and from whom she was divorced March 29, 1836. James Marshall Harding was mayor of Frederick, Justice of the Peace, Sheriff, and Judge of the Orphan's Court. They lived on Patrick Street in Frederick, and he and Sarah had three children. He was head of household in the 1850 census of Fredericktown, with his wife Sarah, and two children at that time. He was then listed as owning two female slaves, one ten years of age, and the other only four. According to the *Jacob Engelbrecht Property and Almshouse Ledgers of Frederick County, Maryland* by Edith Olivia Eader and Trudie David-Long, James M. Harding owned a home on Patrick Street in Frederick, next to that of Gideon Bantz. He sold the property for $4,125 to George Markell on February 22, 1873. The children were:
   a. Edward S. Harding, born March 30, 1842, died December 25, 1923 at his home in Baltimore. Married in York, Pennsylvania January 15, 1867 to Mary E. Wolfe, born c.1843, died August 26, 1923 at Baltimore, daughter of George Wolfe and Eliza Ann Roberts. Edward served in the 3rd Maryland Regiment during the Civil War, and was the father of four children:
      (1) James Edward Harding, born November 8, 1867 and of whom more following.
      (2) George Davis Harding, born October 13, 1869, died February 28, 1920 of pulmonary tuberculosis, and never married.
      (3) Charles Millard Harding, born December 13, 1873, died June 7, 1924 of a carcinoma of the larynx, and never married.
      (4) Mary Grace Harding, born August 22, 1875, died June 26, 1945. Married to Joseph W. Diebert and had one child. Joseph died June 26, 1936 and Mary

married second to Edward Lattin, who died August 17, 1943. Her son was:

(a) Edward Harding Diebert, who died at the age of fourteen from a bowel obstruction.

b. Charles J. Harding, born c.1849; died at about the age of eight.

c. Marshall Fleming Harding, born c.1851, died March 30, 1922; buried at Mt. Olivet Cemetery in Frederick. Married February 7, 1875 to Claire Catherine Smith, and had at least these children:

(1) Elsie May Harding, born May 27, 1900, died January 4, 1945, reportedly at Baltimore. Married March 6, 1924 to James Littleton Morgan, born June 28, 1894, and had at least two children:

(a) Elaine Lillian Morgan, born January 2, 1926 at Baltimore, died June 18, 1994. Married at Pound, Virginia to Foyster Mullins.

(b) James Littleton Morgan, Jr., born February 7, 1928, died November 16, 1990.

(2) James W. Harding.

(3) Edith S. Harding, born c.1896, married to Mealey; buried at Mt. Olivet Cemetery April 29, 1931.

(4) Guy Marshall Harding, born November 20, 1888, died November 23, 1942; buried at Mt. Olivet.

(5) Maude Harding, married to Fink.

(6) Minnie Harding.

(7) Julia Halley Harding.

(8) Lee Harding.

6. Norman Bruce Harding, born June 8, 1812, died March 21, 1873; buried at Mt. Olivet Cemetery in Frederick. Married May 31, 1838 to Maria Ann Ogle, born May 12, 1814, died March 30, 1894; buried at Frederick Catholic Cemetery, daughter of James Ogle, Sr. In the Jacob Engelbrecht Ledgers, Norman Bruce Harding was reported as having been Sheriff of Frederick in 1848. The 1850 census of Fredericktown, as compiled by Mary Fitzhugh Hitselberger and John Philip Dern, published in 1978 under the title *Bridge in Time*, reports a household headed by Nimrod Harding, who we suggest is this same individual. He is there reported as the Sheriff

of the county, born c.1813, with a wife Ann M., born c.1814, and living with them was Mary Ogle, born c.1783, who was probably the mother-in-law, all of which fits this couple. They then had four children:

a. Maria Louisa Harding, born c.1839; married in Frederick April 2, 1861 to Dennis O'Donnohue.
b. Mary E. Harding, born c.1845
c. Alice R. Harding, born c.1847; married in Frederick County, February 4, 1868, to Thomas E. Gonder.
d. Clara E. Harding, born January 23, 1849; died January 26, 1916; buried at Frederick Catholic Church.

7. Louisa Harding, married in Frederick County, October 12, 1848, to Lieutenant Edward Murry, USA.
8. John L. Harding, Jr., born c.1829 in Maryland. In the 1850 census of Fredericktown, listed as a student, living in the household of George Rice (1794), who was an inn-keeper. Married December 7, 1855 to Henrietta Kemp, daughter of Colonel Lewis Kemp. Prior to marriage, he had lived in Gettysburg, Pennsylvania, and some time after marriage, they moved to Missouri, where at least some of the children were born. His children were:
    a. Harald Harding, married the eldest daughter of Colonel Thomas H. Hunt, and lived in Frederick.
    b. Henrietta Harding, born c.1873, died c.1944.
    c. Frank Harding, born c.1861, died c.1865
    d. Eleanor Harding.
9. Eleanora Harding, married in Frederick County February 8, 1861 J. N. Carsanovia.

## James Edward Harding
## 1867-

This son of Edward S. Harding (1842) and Mary E. Wolfe (1843) was born November 8, 1867. His father was a photographer with a business located at 194 Lexington Street in Baltimore, and his mother was a seamstress, working from her home. He married Mary Ignatius McCarthy, daughter of Denis McCarthy and his wife Mary Margaret; both immigrants from Ireland but married in America. The children were:

1. Mary Margaret Harding, born March 17, 1890, died April 7, 1978; single at the time of her death. She had been married, but annulled.
2. Gertrude L. Harding, born July 24, 1891, died May 21, 1973. Married to Lawrence Reil; no children.
3. James Edmond Harding, born September 20, 1893, died August 12, 1948. Married to Rose Cecelia Cronin and divorced after four children. He was married second to Birdy and had four more children:
   a. James Edmond Harding, Jr.
   b. Elizabeth Harding.
   c. Joseph Harding.
   d. Margaret Eleanor Harding.
   e. Jeanne Harding.
   f. Peggy Harding.
   g. Margaret Harding.
   h. Kathleen Harding.
4. Agnes Harding, born January 14, 1896, died September 16, 1973. Married to Thomas Eaton Kinnear, who died July 18, 1972. One child:
   a. Thomas Eaton Kinnear, Jr., married to Barbara Jean Pollock and had five children:
      (1) Sheila Kinnear.
      (2) Mark Kinnear.
      (3) Paul Kinnear.
      (4) David Kinnear.
      (5) Robert Kinnear.
5. Elizabeth Harding, born March 5, 1901, died November 17, 1925 of tuberculosis. She was a nurse, single.
6. Joseph Emmitt Harding, born July 21, 1903, died September 17, 1990; married to Rose and had two children. They were divorced and he married at least three more times. His children were:
   a. Richard Harding, married Helen and had five children.
      (1) Richard Harding, Jr.
      (2) David Harding.
      (3) John Harding.
      (4) Colleen Harding.
      (5) Mary Harding.

b. Bernice Harding, married without children; moved to Arizona.

7. Walter Raleigh Harding, born May 28, 1898; married to Florence Neuenhahan and were divorced after one child. He was married second to Helen Dorothy Ahlfeldt and had children:

a. Elaine Harding, married Homer Works and had children:
   (1) Alisa Works.
   (2) Larry Works.

b. Walter Raleigh Harding, Jr., born December 25, 1938. He was severely injured during his service in the navy and is a quadriplegic.

c. James Edward Harding, born April 3, 1943; married to Barbara Jean Sturgill, born July 21, 1944, who then had a daughter from a prior marriage, who was adopted by James. They then had a son, and later divorced. The children were:
   (1) Robin Harding, born January 4, 1967; married Mark Buellert and had a son:
      (a) Mark Buellert, Jr., born February 27, 1983
   (2) James Edward Harding, Jr., born October 11, 1970. Married c.1990 to Kelly Hammrick. A daughter:
      (a) Jessica Harding, born September 5, 1992

d. Joyce Eileen Harding, born July 29, 1944; married to Richard Marchesani of Rome, New York. Four children:
   (1) Richard Marchesani, Jr.
   (2) Jay Marchesani.
   (3) Dina Marchesani.
   (4) Nikki Marchesani.

# CHAPTER 3

## Elizabeth Harding
## 1758-1823

This daughter of Elias Harding (1728) and Elizabeth Beall (1719), was born c.1758 in a part of Frederick County that later became Montgomery, and died September 1, 1823. Married in the county by license dated January 13, 1778 to Erasmus Perry, born c.1760 in Prince George's County, Maryland, and died March 20, 1826, taken suddenly ill after breakfast, and died that evening. He was a son of Benjamin Perry (1711) and Elizabeth Magruder (1717). In the 1776 census of Prince George's, Erasmus is shown as head of household, with four white males under the age of sixteen; five white females; and twenty-two slaves; a very prosperous planter. According to DAR records, Erasmus served as a private, class 1, in Captain Samuel Swearingen's 5th Co., Colonel John Murdock's Regiment, Lower Battalion, Montgomery County Militia. Under his father's will, he received several slaves: Bambo, Mark, Sauny, Fann, Simon and Ned, and certain furniture and clothes. Upon the death of his mother, he and his two brothers-in-law were to receive her inheritance. He owned part of the tract called *Hermitage,* located at or near Kensington, Montgomery County, which he purchased June 30, 1787 from Thomas Miles. Several members of this family were known to have been buried in a small family cemetery on the home farm. In later years, the property was occupied by the Rock Creek Palisades Elementary School. Four stones were moved at the time and placed flush with the ground on a hill nearby. They had children:

1. Elbert Perry, born c.1782, buried April 29, 1827. Married February 3, 1806 Rebecca Magruder, born c.1788, died March 17, 1856 in Montgomery County. She was a daughter of Ninian Magruder, III (1750) and his first wife, Rachel Cooke. Children:
    a. Erasmus Perry, born November 11, 1806, and of whom more following
    b. Mary Ann Magruder Perry, born February 24, 1808
    c. Eleanora Perry, born June 3, 1810.

d. Elbert Perry, born c.1815, of whom more.

e. Rachel Perry, born c.1817, died July 7, 1883, single

f. Thomas Gassaway Perry, probably, born 1820, died November 12, 1825 with the croup.

2. Benjamin Perry, born c.1785, married February 1, 1804 to Elizabeth Magruder, born c.1786, daughter of Ninian Magruder according to the wording of her will. It was dated April 10, 1863 and proven May 5, 1863; recorded in liber JWS 1 at folio 137 in Montgomery County will records. She names three daughters and two sons in the will, leaving them lands on River Road which "descended to me from my father Ninian Magruder." The reader should note that there was an earlier Elizabeth Magruder, born 1717 and died 1799, whose father was also named Ninian Magruder, but who died in 1751 in what was then Prince George's County. That Elizabeth was married to Benjamin Perry, born 1711. Numerous similarities in these two families, but watch the dates. The library of the Montgomery County Historical Society carries file cards containing transcriptions of the 1850 census for the county. In those files, there is a report of a family apparently headed by Ninian Perry, age 42, who is shown by his mother's will to be a son of Elizabeth. She is in the household, at age 66, as well as: Benjamin F. Perry, age 33; Rachel M. Perry, age 46; Caroline R. Perry, age 22; and Ruth Ann Williams, age 18. The 1860 census for Tenleytown in Montgomery County is confusing. In that report, also transcribed at the library, there is an entry for the household headed by Ninian Perry, with Benjamin F., Elizabeth, Catherine (apparently Caroline) and Ruth in the household. However, in the same census taking for Rockville, the same individuals appear in another household, apparently headed by Philip Suit (with no age given for him). The five just mentioned are there and in addition, there is: Martha Perry, age 49; Amelia Perry, age 21, and James Perry, age 19. From the census records, and the will of Elizabeth, it appears that the children included:

a. Elizabeth Harding Perry, born March 10, 1803.

b. Eleanora Columbia Perry, born c.1816, died April 4, 1890 at the home of her son John. Married April 25,

1846 to Charles Counselman, born c.1807 in Pennsylvania, died February 8, 1889 at the home of his son John in Bethesda. They had children, named in her sister's will, and appeared in the 1850 and 1860 census of the Fourth District:

(1) Benjamin Franklin Counselman, born c.1847

(2) John Mines Counselman, born c.1849

c. Rachel Magruder Perry, November 10, 1804. Her will, dated July 26, 1853, was probated August 26, 1853, and recorded in liber WT of R 2, at folio 244, Montgomery County will records. She was apparently a single lady, leaving her estate to her sisters and brothers.

d. Ninian Magruder Perry, born August 23, 1808, and received a negro boy named Gim under the will of his sister, Rachel M. Perry. This Ninian, of several to bear the name, was perhaps not married. There is a will, dated November 1, 1867, proven February 19, 1889 and filed in liber RWC 15 at folio 213. It was made by Ninian Magruder Perry, and leaves his part of a tract containing seventy-four and one half acres, called *The Resurvey on Honesty* to his brother, Benjamin Franklin Perry. The final papers in the matter were presented to the court by yet another Ninian M. Perry, whom we have yet to properly identify.

e. Erasmus Perry, born October 22, 1809

f. Martha Perry, born c.1811

g. Matilda Perry, born November 3, 1811, died January 4, 1891 in Bethesda. Married in Montgomery County on April 5, 1836 to John Counselman, born c.1805 in Pennsylvania. Head of household in the 1850 census of the Fourth District, they then had seven children. Living with them was Samuel Counselman, born c.1769 in Pennsylvania, probably the father of John. The family next appeared in the 1860 census of the Fourth District, with seven children at home. In the 1870 census of the Fourth District, John owned $6,500 in real estate and $2,000 in personal property, and five of the children were still living at home. In the 1880 census of the Seventh District, Amanda, Hester, Virginia and John were still living at home, single. The children were:

(1) Lucy A. M. Counselman, born c.1837
(2) William G. Counselman, born c.1839
(3) Amanda Counselman, born c.1841; apparently listed as Henrietta in the 1860 census, same age and listed again as Amanda in 1870
(4) Hester A. Counselman, born c.1844; still at home in 1870
(5) Louisa Virginia Counselman, born c.1845; at home in 1870
(6) Hannah E. Counselman, born c.1847; not at home in 1860 or 1870
(7) Benjamin J. Counselman, born c.1849; not at home in 1860, but again listed in 1870
(8) Samuel Counselman, born c.1850
(9) John Counselman, born c.1853, died March 31, 1892 in Bethesda.

h. Benjamin Franklin Perry, born c.1817. In the estate of his sister Rachel M. Perry, he received with his brother, the negro boy, Gim.
i. Caroline R. Perry, born c.1828. Under her sister's will, she received a negro girl, Christy Ann.
j. Ruth Ann Williams Perry, born c.1832
k. Amelia Perry, born c.1839
l. James Perry, born c.1841

3. Basil Magruder Perry; married in Montgomery County by license dated February 10, 1801 to Delilah Elizabeth Waters, born March 16, 1785, died May 12, 1816, daughter of Benjamin Waters (1756) and his first wife, cousin Anne Waters (1758). Basil inherited his mother's share of his father's estate at her death or remarriage, as well as a tract called *Pleasant Hills,* and seven negroes: Aleck, Andrew, Nan, Dick, Davy, Cass and Nick. Delilah was apparently married secondly in the county by license dated January 15, 1810 to John R. Bussard, and had at least one son from her first marriage:
   a. Benjamin Joseph Perry, born February 17, 1803
4. Gassaway Perry, born July 24, 1787, died July 26, 1834. He was Register of Deeds for Montgomery County. Buried at

Rock Creek cemetery in Washington, D. C. Married January 9, 1817 to Sarah Beall, who died May 28, 1842. Children:

a. Augustus Emory Perry, born January 27, 1820 in Rockville, Maryland, died June 16, 1876 of heart failure at his home at 626 F Street, N. W.; buried at Rock Creek Cemetery. Member of the dry goods firm of Perry Brothers in Washington, located on the corner of Pennsylvania Avenue and Ninth Streets, built in 1859. Married in 1844 to Mary Jane Ross, and had five sons and one daughter, including:
   (1) Seaton Perry, born 1850, died January 14, 1898.
   (2) Frank Perry, born c.1858, died June 1, 1860.
   (3) Charles Perry, died January 7, 1883.
   (4) Daughter Perry, married to Dr. William P. Young of Washington, D. C.

b. William Perry.

c. Lewis Perry.

d. Thomas J. S. Perry, born 1825, died September 5, 1881; buried Rock Creek Cemetery. Senior partner of Perry & Co. dry goods merchants.

5. Elias Perry, born 1788, of whom more.

6. Erasmus Perry, Jr., born c.1793, died September 28, 1843. On November 19, 1825, he received from his father the home farm called *Hermitage,* in recognition of his eleven years of management. Married May 8, 1821 to Ruth Ann Williams, born 1802, died August 19, 1888; buried Oak Hill Cemetery, Georgetown. She appears as head of household in the 1850 census for the Berry District of Montgomery County, with five of the children. They had children:

a. John Henry Perry, born c.1822, married December 14, 1859 to Anna M. Senter.

b. Priscilla Marie Perry, apparently a twin, born September 8, 1824, died September 13, 1825

c. Prince Perry, apparently a twin, born September 8, 1824.

d. Richard Humphrey Williams Perry, born 1827, and of whom more.

e. Eden T. Perry, died November 1, 1829

f. William McKendree Perry, born 1828, died August 12, 1871 in Washington, D. C.

g. Charles Wesley Perry, born February 10, 1831, died March 17, 1832
h. Josepheus E. Perry, born March 4, 1832, died May 17, 1855. Married November 21, 1854 to Catherine Niles.
i. James Emory Perry, born July 19, 1835, died August 8, 1837.
j. Rachel Ann Perry, born August 23, 1836, died July 1, 1919. Married January 6, 1859 at the *Hermitage* near Rockville to Henry B. Polkinhorn, born November 23, 1813 in Baltimore, Maryland, died May 29, 1890 in Washington. He had been previously married and had four children. Rachel Ann was mother of one daughter:
   (1) Emma Frances Polkinhorn, born October 23, 1859, died February 22, 1862.
k. Catherine Perry.
l. Benjamin E. Perry, born c.1840, and moved to Missouri c.1856; died June 11, 1892 at his home in Platte City, Missouri. Married to Debrough Coleman (perhaps Deborah).
m. Edwin D. Perry, born c.1842

7. Christiana Perry, married April 3, 1806 Thomas Gittings, born 1786.
8. Rebecca Perry, born c.1798, married June 18, 1827 in Montgomery County to Benjamin B. Dawes. We have seen a report that they moved to Kentucky, which does not appear to be correct. In the 1850 census of the Fourth District, Rebecca was found living in the household of one of her daughters, Muriel Elizabeth, then the wife of Everard Geary Fisher (1824). We have not yet identified other children:
   a. Muriel Elizabeth Dawes, born September 13, 1829 in Montgomery County, and of whom more
9. Priscilla Maria Perry, born July 23, 1799. Married June 4, 1818 to James Pearce.
10. Caroline Perry, born January 23, 1801
11. Elizabeth Perry, born April 11, 1803. Married to Joseph Rose.
12. Matilda Perry, married January 19, 1813 to Edward Beall, or Eden Beall. Children:
   a. William Harrison Beall.
   b. Edward Beall.

## Elias Perry
## 1788-1847

This son of Erasmus Perry (1760) and Elizabeth Harding (1758), was born c.1788 on the family plantation known as *Hermitage,* and died 1847. Married December 14, 1803 to Aquilina Waters, born March 30, 1786, died May 1, 1844, the daughter of Benjamin Waters and his first wife, Anne Waters. Benjamin Waters was born April 12, 1756 at *Jericho* in Prince George's County. He settled on *Three Beall Manor*, which was later within Montgomery County. In the will of Benjamin Waters filed in the latter county, his daughter, Aquilina Perry was left a portion of the tract called *Beall Manor,* and one slave, for the lifetime of her and her husband, and after that, to their children. Thirteen children:

1. Elizabeth Ann Perry, born November 3, 1804.
2. Edmund Perry, born April 27, 1806, died May 8, 1810
3. Caroline Eliza Perry, born December 29, 1808. Married to Isaac Roles, who died c.1832.
4. Erasmus Perry, born 1810.
5. Benjamin Waters Perry, born January 1, 1812, died January 8, 1882. Married first April 11, 1858 to Louisa M. Dorst, born July 18, 1820, died September 17, 1866. Married second October 15, 1867 to Miranda Herndon. Children from first marriage only:
    a. Benjamin Branham Perry, born January 14, 1859, died June 15, 1921. Married July 14, 1886 to Emma L. Broaddus. Children:
        (1) Robert Broaddus Perry; lived at Salina, Kansas. Married Jennie Wilson.
        (2) Benjamin Waters Perry; lived Louisiana. Married Ethel Margaret Baker.
        (3) Lorette B. Perry, single. Lived in Kansas.
        (4) Son Perry, married to Naomie Natalie Monast, and lived in Columbus, Texas.
    b. Louisa Perry, single.
    c. Althea Perry, born 1865. Married June 20, 1900 to Dr. James H. Ross. One daughter:

(1) Louisa Perry Ross. Married Harry George Parker. He taught at Park College, Parksville, Missouri. No children.

6. Thomas Hanson Perry, born November 8, 1813 and died May 17, 1818.
7. John Augustus Perry, born c.1815
8. Charles Alexander Perry, born December 6, 1818, of whom more following.
9. Elias Harding Perry, December 19, 1819 in Montgomery County, Maryland, died December 24, 1890. Married first Elvira H. Perry, born 1828, died June 20, 1851. Married second Anna M., born 1840, died 1929. Child:
   a. May Perry, born May 21, 1865, died January 1, 1956. Married to Branch and had a child:
      (1) Perry W. Branch.
10. Aquilina Maria Perry, born January 19, 1822 (or March 20, 1822). Married to Norris, and moved to the west.
11. Lucretia Matilda Perry, born March 15, 1824. Married to Branch.
12. James William Perry, born c.1826
13. Dorothy Ann Perry, born May 10, 1829. Married to Branch, and moved to St. Joseph, Missouri.

## Charles Alexander Perry
## 1818-1896

This son of Elias Perry (1788) and Aquilina Waters (1786) was born December 6, 1818 in Montgomery County, Maryland, and died September 16, 1896 at St. Joseph, Missouri. Married first September 13, 1842 to Martha Ann Young, born February 22, 1827, died June 6, 1866 in Weston, Missouri. Five children. He married second June 10, 1869 America Elizabeth Hamilton, born February, 1845 at Wilson County, Tennessee, and had four children. His children were:

1. Charles Alexander Perry, Jr., born August 26, 1849, died July 14, 1870
2. Alverda Perry, born January 22, 1852, died May 18, 1932. Married Dr. Craven Jackson.

3. Arcadia Lee Perry, born January 9, 1856, died October 19, 1937. Married George M. Marlowe.
4. Florence Perry, born April 7, 1860
5. William Arthur Perry, born April 20, 1867 and died February 22, 1912; married May Fausnaught. Children:
   a. Florence Perry, born May 21, 1900. Married August 12, 1921 Stanford LaRue Kunkle and had children:
      (1) Stanford LaRue Kunkle, Jr., born May 18, 1922.
      (2) Beverley Ann Kunkle, born February 7, 1924. Married August 23, 1947 to Sam C. Fisher, and had children:
         (a) Craig Scott Fisher: July 25, 1950
         (b) Cherry Lee Fisher: November 2, 1955
         (c) Keith Perry Fisher: July 23, 1959
   b. Martha Perry, born January 4, 1904. Married December 25, 1924 to Arthur G. Zimmerman and had children:
      (1) Janet Perry Zimmerman, born October 26, 1926. Married September 5, 1950 to Robert A. Bosely and had a daughter:
         (a) Cynthia Ann Bosely: October 5, 1956
      (2) Ann Gould Zimmerman, born November 4, 1929. Married June 20, 1950 Randolph D. Bucey, and had a son:
         (a) John Arthur Bucey.
6. John Elias Perry, born May 16, 1870 at Weston, Missouri, died May 12, 1951. Married Josephine Seay, born April 3, 1880 in Smith County, Tennessee. Children:
   a. America Ann Perry, born October 25, 1899
   b. Charles Alexander Perry, born November 26, 1901. Married Josephine Kennedy and had children:
      (1) Charles Alexander Perry, Jr., born 1928. Married Jane Cheney and had children:
         (a) Michael John Perry: March, 1952
         (b) Charles Alexander Perry, III, born December, 1953
         (c) Ann Perry, born 1958
         (d) Daniel Joseph Perry: September 14, 1963
      (2) Joseph H. K. Perry, born 1931. Married December 26, 1959 to Birte Rosenquist in Wilmington, Dela-

ware. Divorced; married second June, 1964 to Regine Jost, in West Berlin, Germany.

   c. Caroline Seay Perry, born December 13, 1903. Married to Cleveland.

7. Benjamin Perry, born August 13, 1874, and an infant death.
8. Robert Hamilton Perry, born September 11, 1872, died 1951. Married to Mai Cecil.
9. America Perry, born September 11, 1871. Married August 28, 1894 to Harvey Truex of St. Louis, Missouri, and had children:
   a. Eldone Hamilton Truex, born August 7, 1896, died April 1, 1919
   b. Rachel Truex, born July 18, 1899. Married April 21, 1928 to Everett Gill, Jr. Children:
      (1) Elizabeth Perry Gill, born September 4, 1929. Married October 13, 1956 Donald Allen White.
      (2) Everett Gill, III, born September 20, 1931;married March 28, 1958 Rachel Louise Granger. One son:
         (a) Stephen Truex Gill.
      (3) Jane Rachel Gill, born February 27, 1933 and married June 15, 1957 Averett Snead Tombes. Two sons:
         (a) Thomas Hamilton Tombes.
         (b) Robert McFarland Tombes.
   c. Aubrey Palmer Truex, born September 14, 1902. Married Martha Miller.

## Richard Humphrey Williams Perry
## 1827-1901

This son of Erasmus Perry, Jr. (1793) and Ruth Ann Williams (1802) was born about May, 1827 in Montgomery County, and died there July 31, 1901. Married October 20, 1870 Margaret Bell Waters, born December 14, 1849, died March 31, 1929, the daughter of John Waters and Elizabeth Ann Cissell, of Montgomery County, Maryland. The family is found in the 1880 census for Montgomery County with four of the children, and again in the 1900 census for Wheaton District of Montgomery County, with four of the children. In 1880, the mother of Richard Humphrey

Williams Perry is living with her son. This family can be used as a good example of checking the accuracy of information. The family was also found in the Ancestral File of the Mormon Church, with just three of the children listed. But, the dates of birth of the parents and all but one of the children was totally inaccurate and misleading. Children:

1. John Waters Perry, born 1872, died December 28, 1877.
2. Walter Early Perry, born November 16, 1875, and died August 12, 1957 at his home in Del Ray Beach, Florida. Married June, 1921 to Sallie Fontaine, born October 2, 1882, died November 20, 1931. Married second June 10, 1934 Willia Green Day, born March 28, 1897 at Weldon, North Carolina, died December 14, 1969 at Del Ray Beach; buried with her husband at the Monocacy Cemetery at Beallsville. Walter Early operated a feed and hardware store in Bethesda for thirty-four years, before retirement. He had been board member and Vice President of the Bank of Bethesda. No children.
3. Mabel Estelle Perry, born August 14, 1877, died January 6, 1949. Married December 31, 1912 to Michael Cunningham Weaver, born 1849, died 1920. Married second Henry Lee. No children. Mabel is listed in the 1900 census, born August, 1877, although that conflicts with the birth date of the following child, who did not appear in the census, having died prior to 1900 as noted.
4. Richard Humphrey Perry, born May 8, 1877, died August 8, 1896.
5. Margaret Elizabeth Perry, born February 17, 1879, died December 10, 1959 of a stroke at Suburban Hospital in Bethesda, Maryland. She was buried at the Monocacy Cemetery, in Beallsville, Maryland. Married as his second wife, to Howard G. Griffith, former postmaster of Silver Spring, born June 22, 1879, died December 27, 1942. They had at least eight children:
    a. Charles Howard Griffith, born August 30, 1907. Married first June 6, 1930 to Mary Beth Terry, born October 15, 1907. He married second July 27, 1946 to Gustava LaMond, born August 30, 1914. One child from the first marriage and two from second:

(1) Charles Howard Griffith, Jr., born October 18, 1931.
(2) James LaMond Griffith, born July 27, 1946
(3) Howard Griffith, born December 28, 1954

b. Margaret Waters Griffith, born January 28, 1910. Married June 20, 1929 to John C. Livingston, born July 5, 1908. Three children:
(1) Elizabeth Ann Livingston, born January 18, 1931. Married April 7, 1955 to Samuel John Irvine, III, born March 9, 1933. Four children:
(a) Samuel John Irvine, IV: May 15, 1956
(b) William Bruce Irvine, born September 24, 1959
(c) Margaret Lee Irvine: October 5, 1961
(d) Laura Irvine, born May 11, 1963
(2) John C. Livingston, Jr., born February 8, 1935 and married September 8, 1956 Carol Frances Shaeffer, born January 24, 1937. Children:
(a) John C. Livingston, III, born November 29, 1958.
(b) Frank William Livingston: March 7, 1962
(c) Terry Suzanne Livingston: July 9, 1963
(3) Howard Griffith Livingston, born October 21, 1941.

c. Mabel Elizabeth Griffith, born January 22, 1912. Married first June 18, 1932 to Townley Gamble, born March 20, 1908, died December 29, 1953. Married second July 19, 1958 to James Hemenway Littlepage, born December 3, 1910. One child from her first marriage; none from the second:
(1) Joan Griffith Gamble, born April 26, 1938. Married September 3, 1960 to James Howe Brown, Jr., and divorced.

d. Thomas Perry Griffith, born January 22, 1913. Married three times: first September 20, 1937 to Lucille Ferris; second to Lorraine Dronenburg, born January 22, 1920, divorced; and third November 4, 1957 to Elizabeth Lochner McNulty. Two children from his first marriage; none from the second; two from the third:

(1) Lucinda Griffith, born September 18, 1938. Married October 7, 1958 to George Walter Sconyers, Jr., born December 16, 1933. Three children:
   (a) George Walter Sconyers, III: July 3, 1959
   (b) Steven William Sconyers: April 11, 1962
   (c) Anne Lucy Sconyers: September 28, 1964
(2) Pamela Griffith, born October 10, 1947
(3) Isobel Griffith, born April 22, 1959
(4) Laura Griffith, born December 14, 1961

e. William Barnstable Griffith, born January 28, 1918. Married April 18, 1947 to Barbara Smith Shetterly, and had a child:
   (1) Mary Patricia Griffith, born May 26, 1948
f. Mary Ann Griffith, born January 15, 1921. Married June 23, 1942 to George Overton Kephart, born February 16, 1920, and had children:
   (1) George Overton Kephart, Jr.: July 7, 1944
   (2) Elizabeth Perry Kephart: November 28, 1945
   (3) Ann Frazer Kephart: April 8, 1949
g. Daughter Griffith, married Morrison M. Clark of Chevy Chase.
h. Daughter Griffith, married Fred Edwards.

6. Benjamin Cissell Perry, born January 7, 1881, died January 10, 1943. He was educated in the public schools of Montgomery and at Columbian University in Washington, now George Washington University, where he graduated from the medical school in 1906. He served for several years in Washington and Baltimore hospitals, and established his practice at Urbana, in Frederick County. In 1929, he was serving as President of the Board of County Commissioners. Married January 26, 1910 to Minnie Lucile Nash, of Frederick County, formerly of St. Louis, Missouri, born April 11, 1886, died 1956. One record found lists her name as Minnie Pappin Nash. She was a daughter of Mrs. Isabelle Nash who, shortly after 1890, purchased the estate known as *Prospect Hall* in Frederick County, where she lived with her three daughters prior to their marriages. The will of Benjamin C. was dated May 29, 1941 and proven January 13, 1943; filed in liber WN 2 at folio 3, Montgomery County will records. It was also

probated April 18, 1944 and recorded in liber RLL 1 at folio 546 in Frederick County. He left one-third of his estate to his widow, and named his two daughters, and his son-in-law. Children:

a. Isabel Tracy Perry, born July 11, 1912. Under her father's will, she received his office building at 6934 Wisconsin Avenue and half interest, with her sister, in property on Old Georgetown Road, known as *Robert's Store*, to be held in trust for her father's sister, Mabel Estelle Perry Lee (1871). This site is believed by the author to be the small general store that still stands a block or two north of Suburban Hospital, a local landmark and still popular. Married three times, second marriage to Hitz, by whom she had a daughter:
    (1) Isabel Perry Hitz, born September 6, 1946
b. Cecil Pappin Perry, born March 1, 1914. Married to Eugene Cassin Carusi, and had children:
    (1) Cecil Perry Carusi, born January 1, 1935, and married to Pierre Pose of Paris, France.
    (2) Lalitte McKaig Carusi, born October 3, 1939. Married June 10, 1961 to Charles Morgan Howell Scott, Lieutenant, USNR.

7. Emma E. Perry, appearing in the 1900 census as having been born February, 1881, although note the conflict with the child listed just previously.
8. Thomas Waters Perry, born October 20, 1883 on the family farm northeast of Kensington, in Montgomery County, Maryland; died October 13, 1962, and was buried at Monocacy Cemetery in Beallsville, Maryland. Married first October 25, 1911 to Alice Emma Weaver, born July 11, 1886, died October 19, 1918, having had three children. Married second October 18, 1924 Mary Alice Allnutt, born February 8, 1900, died September 5, 1990 at Suburban Hospital, and had a child. In Montgomery County, one can not help but recognize this name. This individual is the founder of the T. W. Perry Company, originally The Thomas W. Perry Coal, Oil, Hardware and Lumber Company of Chevy Chase. As he prospered in business, he purchased a farm at Poolesville known as *Briarley*, where he raised Black Angus cattle. He was active

in the politics of the county, and in many civic and business affairs, a member of the Chevy Chase Methodist Church, the Rotary Club, and the Masonic Lodge. He was a director of the Farmers Banking and Trust Company, and a member of the Columbia Country Club. His children were:

a. Marian Weaver Perry, born November 6, 1912. Married October 7, 1933 to Charles Hal Dayhuff, Jr., born December 15, 1907, son of Charles Hal Dayhuff and Monette Duke. Children:
   (1) Marian Alicia Dayhuff, born March 16, 1935. Married first November 26, 1935 to Richard Paxson Youngjohns, born January 13, 1931, and had two children. Married second September 12, 1964 to Colin Hutson; no children. Her two children were:
      (a) Marian Alicia Youngjohns, born August 29, 1954
      (b) Stephanie Jane Youngjohns, born September 12, 1964.
   (2) Charles Hal Dayhuff, III, born October 8, 1937. Married July 2, 1960 Johanna Glass, the daughter of Colonel Robert R. Glass.
   (3) Jane Duke Dayhuff, born April 16, 1940, and married May 23, 1959 to Ronald Wayne Collins. They had children:
      (a) Ronald Wayne Collins, II, born January 13, 1960
      (b) Monette Weaver Collins: May 4, 1961
b. Rachel Ann Perry, born October 25, 1914. Married October 23, 1940 to William Edward Williams, born May 16, 1912, son of William White Williams and Frances Poole. Children:
   (1) William Edward Williams, Jr.: October 3, 1946
   (2) Ann Perry Williams, born January 8, 1949
c. Alice Emma Perry, born April 22, 1917. Married August 21, 1937 Paul Craig Hannum, born August 15, 1908. They had children:
   (1) Carol Ann Hannum, born July 21, 1938. Married February 11, 1961 to James Lamar Minyard, born

October 30, 1932, the son of Bartow David Minyard and Rose Anna Wright and had a son:
(a) Perry Lamar Minyard, born June 18, 1964
(2) Paul Craig Hannum, born August 1, 1940 and married March 24, 1962 Linda Marie Griffin, born May 21, 1940, the daughter of Paul K. Griffin and Wilhemina Dellman. A child:
(a) Christopher Paul Hannum: November, 1962
(3) Mary Alice Hannum, born June 18, 1943 and married October 30, 1964 to David Joseph Price, born August 14, 1943, son of Frank Leib Price and Josephine Sullivan.
(4) Thomas Perry Hannum: September 3, 1950.
d. Thomas Waters Perry, Jr., born December 10, 1925. Married March 25, 1951 Catherine Carter Prescott, born April 16, 1928, the daughter of William H. Prescott and Catherine Carter. In 1963, he was elected to the advisory board of Riggs National Bank, to succeed his father. Children:
(1) Thomas Waters Perry, III: May 13, 1952
(2) Lynn Prescott Perry: September 2, 1953
(3) William Prescott Perry: January 2, 1957
9. Henry Polkinhorn Perry, born 1886, and died October 14, 1889.

## Erasmus Perry
## 1806-1883

This son of Elbert Perry and Rebecca Magruder was born November 11, 1806 in Montgomery County, Maryland, and died November 8, 1883. He and his wife are buried at the United Methodist Church cemetery in Potomac, Maryland. He was married February 27, 1844 to Lydia Elizabeth Fisher, born July 18, 1822, died December 31, 1880, daughter of Thomas Fisher, born January 16, 1782 in England, and Amy Cloud Offutt (1795). They were life-long residents of Montgomery County, and appeared in the 1850 census for the county, with three of their children. In the 1870 census for Brighton Post Office, there are six of the children, and the wife of Thomas Elbert, living in the household. They had children:

1. Thomas Elbert Perry, born February 24, 1845, and died November 8, 1884; buried at Potomac Chapel. Married August 24, 1869 in Frederick County to Marion Alberta Heeter, born December 29, 1848 in Frederick County, and died December 23, 1908 at Potomac, Montgomery County, the daughter of Albert and Lydia C. Heeter of Buckeystown. Buried United Methodist Church at Potomac, Maryland. Thomas Elbert is listed as head of household in the 1880 census of the Fourth District of Montgomery County, listed as a merchant, with his wife and first child. After the death of Thomas Elbert, his widow married secondly May 8, 1895 to Thomas Sullivan, a widower, at Great Falls. He died June 11, 1900, and had children from a prior marriage. Marion Alberta Perry wrote a will dated October, 1887, after the death of her first husband, and before her second marriage. The will was probated February 9, 1909 and recorded in liber HCA 8 at folio 90 in Montgomery County. She named her son and daughter from her first marriage. She also mentions her sister, Elizabeth Cecelia Heeter. In December, 1904, she added a codicil to her will, signing it as Marion Alberta Sullivan. The codicil left the store and room over the store, and the land below, running as far as the hen house, to her son. Thomas Elbert and Marion had children:
    a. Edgar Reed Perry, born May 3, 1871, died August 22, 1935. Married April 27, 1891 to Bertha Louise Ball, born December 29, 1869 in Tioga County, Pa. and died August 19, 1953. They appear in the 1900 census for Potomac District of Montgomery County, with their first child. They had children:
        (1) Ralph Lee Perry, born July 29, 1895. Married April 17, 1920 to Bertha Henry, born October 28, 1897, and had a child:
            (a) Dorie Elva Perry, born September 2, 1925. Married first September 6, 1946 to David Charles Robertson, born June 23, 1923 in Washington, D. C., died November 18, 1950. One child. Married second May 16, 1959 to

Charles Albert Filbey, born January 11, 1909, and had a second child. Children were:

1. Joan Elizabeth Robertson, born November 9, 1947
2. Donna Lynn Filbey, born June 24, 1961

(2) Guy Rayhue Perry, born September 2, 1900. Married first August 29, 1923 to Evelyn R. Stream in Washington, D. C. Divorced, with no children. Married second June 14, 1939 to Mae Carlyle Bonner Strobel, born January 9, 1904. No children.

b. Cora Perry, born March 13, 1881 at Potomac, Maryland, died September 29, 1963. Married November 16, 1898 to John Lewis Ball, born June 6, 1878 in Tioga County, Pa., and died February 8, 1935 at Potomac. This couple is listed in the home of her brother during the 1900 census of Potomac District, of Montgomery County, with a child:

(1) Anson L. Ball, born September, 1899.

2. Ninian M. Perry, born May 26, 1847, died March 16, 1923. Married February 12, 1877 to Hannah A. Dailey, born c.1856 in Virginia, died October 20, 1899. Ninian appears as head of household in the 1880 census for Montgomery County, with his wife, and their first son. He appears again in the 1900 census for the Bethesda District of Montgomery County, apparently widowed, with six of his children. His will, dated March 9, 1923, was proven March 22, 1923 and filed in liber HCA 26 at folio 402 in Montgomery County will records. His wife predeceased him, and he had apparently been married secondly to Jane B. H., whom he mentions as "my late wife." The will of Jane B. H. Perry was probated May 31, 1922 and filed in liber HCA 26 at folio 248. She named as her heirs three nieces: Gertrude, Florence and Edith Manship, who were to receive her cottage on River Road and ten acres, the property in which her sister, Grace Osborne, then lived. There was no mention in her will of any husband or children. The will of Ninian M. Perry named his children, with specific bequests:

a. Albert A. Perry, born September 14, 1879, and died April 28, 1940. Married to Mary E., born January 31, 1882 and died July 21, 1959.
b. Josephus Perry. This child appears in the Soundex for the 1900 census reading as Josephine Perry, born January, 1881, but has not been verified.
c. John Ninian Perry, born April 24, 1883, died October 9, 1940. Married to Rose A., born April 3, 1870, died December 17, 1938. This is apparently the same John Ninian Perry, whose will was dated August 20, 1940 and probated October 23, 1940; recorded in liber HGC 33 at folio 281, Montgomery County will records. However, the will names a wife as being Gertrude Ruth, who received his entire estate, and may be a second marriage after the death of Rose A. as noted. At least one son:
   (1) Horace M. Perry, born October 26, 1907, and perhaps an early death.
d. Noble F. Perry, born January, 1885 and died 1965. Married to his first cousin, Myrtle E. Perry, born 1892, died 1955, daughter of Erasmus Perry, Jr. (1858) and Rebecca Eveley, and had children.
e. Hannah Bertha Perry, born January, 1889; married to Husband.

3. Mary Ann Perry, born c.1849; married September 19, 1871 to Samuel Duvall. In *Genealogical Abstracts, Montgomery County Sentinel 1855-1899,* the groom's name is listed as Samuel Denall, apparently incorrect.
4. Henry Clay F. Perry, born April 3, 1852, died November 6, 1918. Married March 5, 1884 to Vandelia Heeter, of Frederick, born August 21, 1855, died March 6, 1912. Both buried at United Methodist Church, Potomac. In the 1900 census for Bethesda, Montgomery County, her birth year is listed as 1858. One son in the census:
   a. Bernard Clay Perry, born October, 1885, died 1955.
5. Eleanor Perry, born c.1855
6. Erasmus Perry, Jr., born February 15, 1858, died February 11, 1920. Married Rebecca Eveley. At least one son, buried with his parents at United Methodist Church in Potomac. They appear in the 1900 census for Bethesda, in Montgomery

County, Maryland, with three of their children. The known children were:

a. Thomas Elbert Perry, born 1887, died 1918.
b. Virgie Perry, born December, 1885
c. Thomas Perry, born February, 1887
d. Myrtle E. Perry, born August, 1892 and died 1955. Married her first cousin, Noble F. Perry, born 1885, died 1965, son of Ninian M. Perry (1847) and Hannah A. Dailey (1856), and had children.

7. Lydia Elizabeth Perry, born c.1859. Married September 11, 1888 in Rockville, Maryland, to Charles H. Mathews. At least one son:

a. Clarence H. Mathews, born 1889, died 1918

## Elbert Perry
## 1815-1888

This son of Elbert Perry (1782) and Rebecca Magruder (1788) was born October 22, 1815 in Montgomery County, Maryland, died September 4, 1888; buried Darnestown Presbyterian Church. Married February 23, 1848 in Montgomery County, to his cousin, Elizabeth Rebecca Clagett, born December 3, 1820, and died February 17, 1880, buried with her husband. This is apparently the couple found in the 1850 and the 1860 census for Rockville, Montgomery County, with Elbert shown as born about 1815/16 and Elizabeth born c.1821/24. In the 1850 census, there is also Rebecca Perry at age 61, born c.1789, living in the household, who is apparently the mother of Elbert. Six children listed with them in the census:

1. William E. Perry, born July 21, 1851, died October 26, 1886 and buried with his parents. According to obituary in the *Sentinel,* he left a wife and several small children. He is perhaps the same William E. who was married in the county, December 5, 1872 to Mary A. Offutt.
2. John Perry, born c.1854
3. Susan Perry, born c.1856
4. Richard Perry, born c.1857

5. Amanda Perry, born c.1859. Perhaps the same Amanda who was married at the Darnestown Presbyterian Church November 23, 1883 to Peyton D. Vinson.
6. Barbara Perry, born c.1860
7. Elbert Perry, Jr., shown in the 1870 census of the family. Records of the Darnestown Presbyterian Church report his baptism February 13, 1887, listed as Elbert Perry, Jr. and an adult at the time. He is perhaps the same Elbert who is buried at Darnestown Presbyterian Church with other family members, born September 14, 1861, and died February 9, 1928. Married March 17, 1891 to Lillie Clagett, born c.1863, died July 14, 1944 in Washington. The couple appear in the 1900 census for Gaithersburg, Montgomery County, Maryland, with three of their children. They were parents of, at least:
   a. Nathaniel C. Perry, born December, 1893, of Washington, D. C. (1944)
   b. Elizabeth Eleanor Perry, born August, 1895, and baptized at the Darnestown Presbyterian Church, September 3, 1899. Died March 6, 1979, single.
   c. Arthur Lee Perry, born September, 1897, baptized at Darnestown Presbyterian Church September 3, 1899, of Wilmington, Delaware (1944)

**Muriel Elizabeth Dawes**
**1829-**

This daughter of Benjamin B. Dawes and Rebecca Perry (1798) was born September 13, 1829 in Montgomery County. She was married there November 28, 1844 to Everard Geary Fisher, born January 19, 1824, and died June 12, 1870, son of Thomas Fisher (1782) and Amy Cloud Offutt (1795). Everard was head of household in the 1850 census of the Fourth District of Montgomery County, with his wife and three children at home. Living with them was Rebecca Dawes, born c.1798, probably Muriel's mother. The family next appeared in the 1860 census for the Rockville District, with him listed as E. G. Fisher, using his initials. There were then five children at home. He was married second August 18, 1869 to Mary Eliza West, born c.1835, and had one child from that marriage. The 1870 census of the Fourth District listed Eliza as head of household, with Edward G. Fisher also listed there. There was one infant child listed in the household. In the 1900 census of the Sixth District, Eliza was a widow, living in the household of Amos West (1842) and listed as a sister. With her was her daughter Marion, listed as a niece of Amos. The children from both marriages of Edward Gary Fisher were:

1. Alcesta Ann Fisher, born c.1847. Married December 23, 1863 to Julian Osmond, born September, 1837 in Louisiana. They were first found in the 1870 census for the First District of Montgomery County, with three children. Living with them was Isadora W. Fisher, born c.1861, whom we have not yet identified, but is probably a daughter of one of the brothers of Alcesta Ann. Julian appeared as a widower in the 1880 census for the Fourth District, with six children at home. Perhaps we transcribed the census incorrectly, but after the listing of the six children appeared the name Alcestra Osmond, born c.1847, but said to be a sister. However, in the 1900 census for the Fourth District, we again found Julian and Alceser A., listed as married, with two children and two grandchildren at home. They were said to have been married for thirty-six years, having had twelve children, eight of them then living. The children included:
    a. Julian E. Osmund, born c.1866 in the District of Columbia. In the 1880 census of the Fourth District, living in the household of Harriett Rolison (1837). Married January 25, 1890 to Clara Eva Dwyer, born February, 1860, daughter of Henry Pierce Dwyer (1820) and Catharine Benson (1821). Julian was head of household in the 1900 census for the Potomac District, with wife Clara E. and two sons, both born in the District of Columbia:
        (1) Aubrey Osmond, born May, 1891.
        (2) Franklin J. Osmond, born September, 1895.
    b. Benjamin Osmund, born c.1868 in Maryland. This child is listed as Webster in the 1880 census, perhaps a middle name, but the proper age.
    c. Mary L. Osmund, born c.1870 in Maryland; at home in 1880 and 1900, single.
    d. Rhoda Osmund, born c.1871. The full name of this child was Lelia Rhoda Osmund, married September 24, 1894

to Richard H. Florance. In 1900, she was living in her parents' household, with two sons:

(1) Henry R. Florance, born June, 1895

(2) Hazel Florance, born July, 1896

e. Alcestra Osmund, born c.1874

f. Inez Osmund, born c.1877

g. Frances Osmund, born c.1879

h. Belle Perry Osmund, infant death September 5, 1884

2. Millard Clay Fisher, born November 20, 1848, died April 23, 1918, buried in the St. Mary's Catholic Cemetery near Rockville with his wife. He was born a Methodist and converted to the Catholic religion, baptized October, 1916 at St. Mary's in Rockville. Married May 20, 1871 to Mary Elizabeth Boswell, born November 6, 1848, died October 26, 1932, daughter of Alexander Franklin Boswell (1818) and Mary Elizabeth Beckwith (1824). Millard was head of household in the 1880 census of the Fourth District, and they had six children at that time. Next found in the 1900 census of the Potomac District, with ten children at home. They had been married twenty-three years, having had thirteen children, with twelve then living. Children were:

a. John Franklin Millard Fisher, born February 29, 1872, died December 15, 1935; not at home in 1900. This is apparently John F. Fisher, found in the 1900 census living next door to his father Millard. John F. was married December 27, 1893 to Dovie Catherine Anders, born August, 1872, daughter of William Anders. In 1900 they had three children, and there were more born later:

(1) Marie J. Fisher, born January, 1895. Perhaps the same who was married June 6, 1917 at St. Mary's Catholic Church to Philip Reed of Rockville.

(2) Glenna Elizabeth Fisher, born September 13, 1896. Married at St. Mary's Catholic Church, Rockville, October 11, 1923, William Carol Carhart, the son of William and Maria Carhart of Washington, District of Columbia.

(3) Millard M. Fisher, born November, 1898

(4) Charles F. Fisher, died October 5, 1972 at Hollywood, Florida. His obituary mentions several sisters

by their married names, and his brother, the late Millard Fisher, identifying his position in this family. The married sisters were: Mrs. William C. Carhart; Mrs. R. M. Powell; Mrs. Selby P. Reffitt; Mrs. Frank C. Riley; Mrs. Clyde Richardson; and Mrs. Rupert Hughes. Note that the marriages of the two eldest daughters in this family above are reported; the remaining five younger daughters appear to be married to the individuals just listed, although we can not now identify which. Married to Margaret E. and had at least three daughters:

(a) Daughter, married to William P. Hilton.
(b) Daughter, married to John A. Smith.
(c) Daughter, died before 1972; married to Edward J. Kuzas.

(5) Belva Romaine Fisher, born November 5, 1903.
(6) Ruth Adelaide Fisher, born April 13, 1907
(7) Ella William Fisher, born May 15, 1910. Records of St. Mary's Catholic Church, Rockville.
(8) Dorothy Lee Fisher, born December 5, 1912.
(9) Margaret Lee Fisher, born January 31, 1915

b. Geary Aloysius Fisher, born February 7, 1873, and of whom more following.

c. Mariel Genevieve Fisher, born October 30, 1874, died July 10, 1963. Married May 23, 1908 to John Henry Miller, but had no children.

d. William Thomas Fisher, born August 2, 1876, died June 1, 1907, listed as a portable engineer in the 1900 census. Married at St. Mary's Catholic Church in Rockville, on September 26, 1900 to Agnes Eugenia Thrift, born January, 1877, daughter of Charles Henry Thrift (1836) and Mary A. McCrossin (1848). The paternal grandfather of Charles Henry Thrift was Absalom Thrift, of Welsh ancestry; his maternal grandfather was John Rabbitt, who emigrated from England as a young man. At least one child was born:

(1) Anna Lucille Fisher, born December 5, 1902. Baptized March 6, 1903, St. Mary's Catholic Church at Rockville.

e. Cecelia Elizabeth Fisher, born February 19, 1878, died August 5, 1881.

f. Isadora Teresa Fisher, born February 16, 1880, died May 9, 1944. Records of St. Mary's Catholic Church in Rockville list this child as Ida Theresa Fisher, with the proper birth date. Married September 28, 1904 to James E. Cavanaugh. In the 1900 census, there is a daughter whose name appeared to be Ira T. as we transcribed the census, born April, 1880, which is perhaps this same child. There was at least one son, mentioned in the obituary of his grandmother:

    (1) John Cavanaugh, in 1932 a student in the Seminary of Foreign Missions at Maryknoll, New York.

g. Eva Stella Fisher, born April 20, 1881, died October 6, 1972. Married April 20, 1918 to John G. Willier.

h. Joseph Eldridge Fisher, born January 1, 1883, died March 24, 1919. Married September 20, 1910 to Mary E. McAvoy. At least one daughter, in records of St. Mary's Catholic Church. Those reports are more often than not written in Latin versions of the names, and it is my understanding that two given names are sometimes reversed, so that the name of the Saint appears first. We found also an obituary of one individual, whom we believe to be a son of this family. The children included:

    (1) Joseph E. Fisher. According to his obituary in the *Gazette* newspaper, Joseph was born c.1914 in Rockville, and died November 21, 1998 at St. Michaels, Maryland, and was formerly of Gaithersburg. Buried with military honors at Maryland Veterans Cemetery at Hurlock, Maryland. He was for many years employed by Atlantic Seaboard Corporation as a supervisor of underground installation of pipe lines across the country. He was the leader of Montgomery County 4-H Beef Club and 4-H Superintendent of the Montgomery County Fair. During World War Two, he was commissioned a Second Lieutenant, and served with General Patton across Europe; discharged to the Army Reserve as a Lieutenant Colonel. His wife was Elizabeth S. and

he was survived by a sister, Mrs. Cecelia F. Cissel and six grandchildren. Two sons:

(a) Thomas M. Fisher of Salisbury in 1998

(b) Richard L. Fisher, living in McLean, Virginia in 1998

(2) Cecelia Elizabeth Fisher, born October 29, 1919; married to Cissel.

i. Albert Ambrose Fisher, born March 24, 1884, died July 19, 1884.

j. Elizabeth Delight Fisher, born May 25, 1885, died November 14, 1968. Records of St. Mary's Catholic Church in Rockville list her birth as March 24, 1885, and state that her father was non-Catholic. The 1900 census lists Gussie D. Fisher, a daughter, born May, 1885, which is apparently this child. Married February 22, 1917 William P. Doyle.

k. Mary Margaret Fisher, born February 22, 1887, died August 20, 1964. Married October 1, 1928 to Edward P. Watson, the son of Edward and Catherine Watson. There were no children.

l. Stanley Eustace Fisher, born November 23, 1889, died November 18, 1969. Married at Holy Trinity Church in Washington September 18, 1937 to L. Gladys McClellan; no children.

m. Leland Lawrence Fisher, born April 3, 1891 at Potomac, died January 2, 1969 at his home in Rockville. Married December 9, 1914 to Erma Helen Maria Bogley, born October 1, 1888, died February 26, 1971, daughter of William A. Bogley and Isabel Haney. In 1916, he began office work for the Oscar L. Johnson Lumber Company in Rockville, which he purchased in 1948, and renamed it the Leland L. Fisher Lumber Company. Leland was a fellow member of the Rockville Lions Club with this author, and a former president of the club. They had one daughter:

(1) Helen Marie Fisher, born November 14, 1919 at Rockville. Married first to Hershey by whom she had two children, and second to Ray Weddle of Rockville. Her children were:

(a) Richard M. Hershey.
(b) Donald J. Hershey.

n. James Spencer Fisher, born November 16, 1894, died December 4, 1960. Married November 22, 1916 Frances Butler; no children. Records of St. Gabriel's Catholic Church at Potomac list this child as Jacobum Spencer (Latin form) or Jacob Spencer Fisher.

3. Mariel Editha Fisher, born May 30, 1850; two days old at the time the census was taken. This child appears to be listed as Mary in the 1860 census. Married in the county by license dated July 7, 1868 to her cousin, Edmund Ernest Fisher, born c.1842, son of Samuel M. Fisher (1815) and Louisa Benton (1814). He and Mary, born c.1850, were found in the 1870 census of the Fourth District, where he was listed as a lock keeper on the canal. Living with them was Everett G. Fisher (sic), born c.1855, also a lock keeper, who is more correctly Everard Geary Fisher, Jr., his cousin, and brother of his wife. In the 1880 census of the Fourth District, we found the household of E. E. Fisher, born c.1842, who would appear to be this individual. However, his wife is there listed as Dethia, born c.1847, which could be a second marriage or a misinterpretation of her name. There were then three children at home. In the 1900 census for the Potomac District, we found the household of Edward Fisher (rather than Edmund) of the proper age, having perhaps misread the entry, a canal laborer. His wife was Mary E. of the proper age, which rules out the possibility of a second marriage discussed just above. There were then three children at home, one of them being a widow with her two small children. The census reports that Edward (Edmund) and Mary E. have been married for 32 years, and have had ten children, six of them still living. The children appear to have included, at least:

a. May Fisher, born c.1870
b. Samuel Edmund Fisher, born c.1872; baptized August 9, 1897, Rockville Methodist Church.
c. Annie Fisher, born c.1874
d. Annie Emma Agnes Fisher, born October, 1876; baptized in the Rockville Methodist Circuit on August 9, 1879. Married December, 1893 to Samuel T. Anderson;

living at home with her parents in 1900, widowed, having had three children, two still living with their mother:
   (1) Maywood E. Anderson, female, born August, 1894
   (2) Samuel A. Anderson, born May, 1897

e. Mary Magnolia Fisher, infant baptism August 9, 1879 at Rockville Methodist Church. She was born April 23, 1871 at Great Falls in Montgomery County, and died February 12, 1926. Married in Washington March 23, 1892, to John William Bissett, born March, 1868 in Maryland, died August 12, 1912 at Great Falls. He was head of household in the 1900 census of the Potomac District, listed as an aqueduct laborer, with his wife Mary M., married for eight years. She had been mother of five children, three of them surviving, and at home. At least one more child was born after the census taking:
   (1) Cora I. Bissett, born April, 1892
   (2) John E. Bissett, born September, 1894
   (3) William D. Bissett, born August, 1897
   (4) James Ernest Bissett, born March 14, 1905 at Great Falls, died August 25, 1985. Married April 29, 1924 at Alexandria, Virginia to Blanche June Hebb, born October 10, 1905, and had at least one daughter:
      (a) Beverly June Bissett, born March 26, 1925 at Washington; married there November 23, 1946 to Carl Franklin Kauffman, born May 10, 1917 in Manor Township, Lancaster, Pennsylvania.

f. James Fisher, perhaps, born March, 1881. In 1900, he was living two dwellings removed from that of this family, listed as a farm laborer with Richard Gray (1876).

g. Thomas V. Fisher, born February, 1884; in 1900 a ferry laborer.

h. Eva Editha Fisher, born May 28, 1887

4. Everard Geary Fisher, Jr., born c.1851. In the 1860 census of Rockville District, we found E. G. Fisher living in the household of George P. Atwood (1792). We then found a marriage license dated June 27, 1877 between Everard G. and Constantia Fisher. She appears to be the same individual born c.1854, daughter of Samuel M. Fisher (1815) and Louisa Benton (1814). Finally, in the 1880 census for the Fourth District, in

household #212, there are E. G. Fisher and his wife Constantia living with Arthur Fisher and his wife Elizabeth, whom we believe to be his brother Artaxerxes, as discussed below; forming the basis for our assumption that this Everard belongs in the family, despite the fact that in the 1860 census, his birth year would have been 1851, and in the 1880 census, it would have been calculated at 1855. Also listed with the two Fisher couples was John Henderson (1856) and his wife Anna Henderson (1860). The 1880 census is a bit confusing, in that we also found in the Fourth District household # 341, headed by John Henderson and his wife (there listed as Hannorah), with a son William Henderson (1878). Living with them are Everard (there listed as Everet) and his wife Constantia. He is listed as a lock tender, and they have a child Ella L. with them. We can only assume that there was some movement during the taking of the census and these individuals were counted twice. In the 1900 census, Constantia appears as head of household, with her husband listed as Everet G., a canal worker and five children. We can identify with some certainty the following:

a. Samuel Millard Fisher, baptized November 7, 1878. St. Mary's Catholic Church, Rockville, with the notation "outside the church". The parents are recorded as Evert G. and Constance Fisher of Montgomery County. This child was not found in any census record.
b. Helen Lane Fisher, born December 31, 1879; baptized June 9, 1880, St. Mary's Catholic Church, Rockville. This is apparently the child listed as Ella L. in the 1880 census.
c. Mary Rose Fisher, born August 8, 1882; perhaps the same who was married September 26, 1900 to Francis E. Ricketts at Rockville Methodist Church.
d. Emma Viola Fisher, born c.1885, died September 28, 1886 at Great Falls.
e. Louis M. Fisher, born November, 1886
f. Mariel Fisher, born July, 1888
g. Lee R. Fisher, born July, 1890

5. Martha Fisher, born c.1852. This could possibly be the Martha who was married to James W. Benson, born c.1845 and

appears with him in the 1880 census for the Clarksburg District. However, she is there listed as 33 years of age (born c.1847), five years different from the earlier census reports. Living with them is Mary Fisher, listed as sister-in-law, at the age of 20 years (born c.1860). See just above a sister Mariel or Mary, middle name Edista, but clearly born c.1850. This is the only sister combination of Martha and Mary we have found in this time period, despite the birth year differences.

6. Artaxerxes Fisher, born c.1860, died January 28, 1900. This individual is believed to be the same as Arthur Fisher, of the approximate same birth year, found as head of household in the 1880 census for the Fourth District, with a wife Elizabeth, born c.1863. There was a marriage in the Rockville Methodist Circuit, dated July 15, 1879 between Artaxerxes Fisher and Elizabeth A. Carey, which would appear to be the couple. He was then said to be twenty-one years of age, and she was seventeen. She appears to have been the daughter of John T. Carey (1822) found in the 1870 census of the Third District with a wife and children, including Elizabeth of the proper age. Living with the couple was E. G. Fisher and his wife Constantia, which we believe to be his brother Everard G. Fisher, Jr. as discussed above. There is another couple living in the household in 1880, not yet identified as to relationship, if one exists: John Henderson, born c.1856 in Maryland, and Anna Henderson, born c.1860 in the District of Columbia. In the 1900 census of the Potomac District, we found a household headed by Elizabeth Fisher, a widow, there said to have been born April, 1851 with seven children at home. They were living next door to the household of Constantia Fisher, also widowed, who had married Everard G. Fisher, Jr., as discussed above. We note that these two couples had lived together, and it appears probable that the two widows are still living near each other. The one problem with this assumption is that Elizabeth is listed in 1900 as having been born in 1851, which is ten years earlier than other tabulations. Subject to verification, we suggest the possibility of an error in transcribing the census (by this same author). All known facts point to this being the Elizabeth A. Carey who was the widow of Artaxerxes Fisher (1860). Children were:

a. Maud Elizabeth Fisher, born August 19, 1882. Her birth record from Rockville Methodist Church lists her parents as Artaxerxes E. and Ann Fisher. Apparently the same Maud who was married September 5, 1900 to David W. Ricketts.
b. Ida M. Fisher, born September, 1884
c. Ernest E. Fisher, born August, 1886; married March 1, 1905 to Ruth E. Kidwell.
d. Laywood L. Fisher, born July, 1888
e. Percy Fisher, born May, 1890
f. Rossey Fisher, a son, born July, 1894
g. Isaac U. Fisher, born May, 1896

7. Emma Delight Fisher, born December 16, 1862, died March 13, 1954. Married June 8, 1880 at the Cromelin House, Great Falls, to Charles Absalom Case, born September, 1857, son of George W. Case (1825) and Elizabeth Jane Thrift (1828). They were found in the 1900 census of the Potomac District, married 20 years, and the parents of three children, all living, and at home. Also living with them was Ellen J. Case, born October, 1827, mother of Charles; and William H. Case, born September, 1859, a farm laborer; and Samuel T. Case, born November, 1864, a carpenter; both being brothers of Charles. The children were:
   a. George D. Case, born July, 1881
   b. Charles S. Case, born April, 1884
   c. Mary E. Case, born May, 1888
8. Marion Fisher, born c.1870 to the second marriage

## Geary Aloysius Fisher
## 1873-1924

This son of Millard Clay Fisher (1848) and Mary Elizabeth Boswell (1848) was born February 7, 1873, and died September 13, 1924 of cholera morbus and ptomaine poisoning; buried in the new cemetery, St. Mary's Church. Married November 25, 1897 at St. Mary's Parsonage in Rockville to Martha Mary Connelly of Layhill, born April 10, 1874, died June 24, 1945, daughter of Thomas Jefferson Connelly (1846) and Anna Frances Maryum

King (1849). Geary A. served as first president of the Montgomery County Game and Fish Protective Society. Eleven children:

1. Helen Agatha Fisher, born August 11, 1898; died May 14, 1983. Married May 17, 1923 to Joseph Oscar Matthews, born March 17, 1901; died July 30, 1970. Four children:
   a. Mary Claire Matthews, born July 28, 1924. Married Yves Joseph Ogaard, born October 1, 1920; children:
      (1) Elizabeth Jeanne Ogaard, born February 11, 1951
      (2) Helen Cecilia Ogaard, born November 9, 1953
      (3) Anthony Ogaard, born 1954 infant death
      (4) Mary Caron Anne Ogaard born September 4, 1956
   b. Joseph Oscar Matthews, Jr., infant death December 26, 1925
   c. Joseph Oscar Matthews, Jr., born March 1, 1929
   d. Barbara Anne Matthews, born August 8, 1931, married April 8, 1955 George Joseph Hranicky. Children:
      (1) Teresa Anne Hranicky, born February 15, 1956, died May 6, 1979 in Silver Spring, Maryland
      (2) Justine Claire Hranicky: June 30, 1957
      (3) Thomas Jerome Hranicky: November 1, 1958
      (4) Kenneth Bede Hranicky: July 27, 1961
   e. John Barry Matthews, born September 6, 1933. Married September 1, 1956 Margaret Kennedy Keane, born September 13, 1934. They had children:
      (1) John Barry Matthews, Jr., born August 26, 1957
      (2) Margaret Keane Matthews, born October 5, 1958
      (3) Susan Fisher Matthews, born October 17, 1959
      (4) Steven Kennedy Matthews.
2. Mary Caroline Fisher, born August, 1900, an infant death
3. Evelyn Aloysius Fisher, born February 24, 1902; died November 10, 1959. Married February 11, 1929 to Roy Charles Arehart, born August 27, 1905; died January 8, 1986. At least one son:
   a. Thomas Mitchell Arehart, born August 8, 1930. Married August 31, 1951 to Lucille Yvonne O'Neal, born 1936; and had children:
      (1) Patricia Michelle Arehart, born May 30, 1957
      (2) Charles Michael Arehart, born June 4, 1962
      (3) Tracey Ann Arehart, born June 1, 1963

4. Lawrence Prescott Fisher, born March 18, 1903, died February 1, 1958 in Rockville. Married April 24, 1934 to Rose Camille Kirkland, born October 29, 1902. One son:
   a. Geary Lawrence Fisher, born December 4, 1940; perhaps the father of twins:
      (1) Patrick Geary Fisher.
      (2) William Michael Fisher.
5. Andrew Geary Fisher, born April 7, 1904; died December 22, 1983. Married April, 1929 Sarah Bridget Costello, born September 2, 1903, and died October 4, 1967. One daughter, adopted:
   a. Mary Elsa Fisher.
6. Joseph Milton Fisher, born August 18, 1905; died March 18, 1981. Married October 21, 1933 at St. Mary's Church Rockville, Janet Faville Armstrong, born June 28, 1910, daughter of Hugh Armstrong, and had children:
   a. Lawrence Gregory Fisher, born March 4, 1936. Married April 30, 1968 Louisa Elko, born January 21, 1939
   b. Robert Edward Fisher, born October 21, 1940
   c. Stanley Albert Fisher, born November 12, 1944
   d. Douglas Vincent Fisher, born October 17, 1947
7. Jessie Theckla Fisher, born August 22, 1907; died December 14, 1972. Married October 8, 1942 to Forest Milburn George, born 1903 and died July, 1952. Children:
   a. Michael Clair George, born July 16, 1943
   b. Sarah Gail George, born October 9, 1945
   c. Elizabeth Ann George, born May 2, 1947
8. John Norman Fisher, born March 30, 1908; died March 26, 1950 at his home on Madison Street in Bethesda. Buried at St. Mary's Cemetery, Rockville. Married November 11, 1939 Anna Marie Fannon, born 1912. Children:
   a. John Norman Fisher, Jr., born October 3, 1941; perhaps the father of two children:
      (1) Allison Fisher.
      (2) John Warren Fisher.
   b. Linda Anne Fisher, born May 18, 1946
   c. Mary Constance Fisher, born October 1, 1949
9. Philip Adrian Fisher, born April 1, 1912; died December 24, 1982. Baptized April 13, 1912, St. Mary's Catholic Church,

Rockville. Married Celestine Dominowski, born November 3, 1923, and had children:

a. Leslie Ann Fisher, born May 21, 1952
b. Michael Alan Fisher, born August 19, 1954
c. Nancy Lee Fisher.

10. Mary Edna Fisher, known as "Nook", born July 13, 1913. Married October 21, 1939 to Frank John Nivert, born October 18, 1915, and had children:
    a. Frank John Nivert, Jr., born May 21, 1942
    b. Mary Catherine Nivert, born October 25, 1944. Married February 27, 1972 to William Thomas Danoff and had children:
        (1) Emma Seton Danoff: October 26, 1975
        (2) Lucy Caroline Danoff: January 26, 1979
    c. Edward Joseph Nivert, born January 5, 1947
11. Thomas Warren Fisher, born August 22, 1921. Following in the conservation footprints of his father, T. Warren twice served as president of the Rockville chapter of the Izaac Walton League, and one year as state president. In January of 1998, he received the Wildlife Conservation Award from the Maryland-Delaware Chapter of the Wildlife Society for "significant contributions to resource management and conservation, his high degree of organizational effort, leadership and participation in management and resource programs." Married 1948 to Lois Jean Foster, born April 14, 1926 and died January 24, 1964, and had the first three children listed. She was buried at Gate of Heaven Cemetery, Aspen Hill, Montgomery County, and was the daughter of Colonel Roy M. Foster and Gladys Griffith of Lake Helen, Florida at the time of her death. Thomas Warren Fisher was married second February 2, 1966 Sheila Ann Marie Hall (or Hill), born January 30, 1943, and had the last daughter:
    a. Lois Ann Fisher, born May 10, 1949; married Covati and had children:
        (1) Stephanie Amber Covati.
        (2) Matthew Warren Covati.
    b. Christine Lee Fisher, born April 17, 1951
    c. Patricia Marie Fisher, born June 27, 1955; married John Patrick Morris, born September 29, 1954, son of Harold

Clayton Morris (1923) and Jean Evelyn Burdette (1927); and had children:

(1) Joseph Guy Morris, born 1989

(2) Andrew Madison Morris, born 1991

d. Elizabeth Catherine Fisher.

# CHAPTER 4

## John W. Harding
## 1789-1861

John W. Harding was born February 16, 1789 in Montgomery County, Maryland, and was a farmer, living in the area of the Sandy Spring Post Office. He died before September 3, 1861 when his will was probated in the county. It was written September 25, 1855 and is recorded in liber JWS 1 at folio 90. In his will, his wife is not named, but there are references to at least nine children and a grandson. He was listed in the 1850 census of the Fifth District as John Hardin (sic), of the proper age. His wife Sarah was present, and they had living with them their youngest son, Andrew Jackson (there listed only as Jackson), and a grandson, Zachariah Hardin (sic), then eleven years old; son of Asbury Harding. They were then living next door to son Joseph, whose surname was also spelled Hardin by the census taker. John was a slave owner, reported with three in the 1850 census. He then owned 80 acres of improved land and 820 acres unimproved, at $4,500 total value. He owned 4 horses, 3 milch cows, 6 other cattle, and 25 swine. In the previous year he had produced 150 bushels of wheat, 20 bushels of rye, 500 bushels of Indian corn, 50 bushels of Irish potatoes, 100 pounds of butter, and 3 tons of hay.

Head of household in the 1860 census of the Fifth District of Montgomery County, he had a wife Sarah, born c.1793 in Maryland, and they then had two sons at home. Living with them was James Johnson, born c.1846, and Rachel Graham, born c.1828. According to family group sheets found in the Historical Society library at Rockville, John was perhaps married to Sarah E. Moore, born c.1788, and perhaps died December 24, 1825. All born in Montgomery County, the children included:

1. Mary Harding, born December 24, 1810; in her father's will referred to as Mary Key.
2. Samuel R. Harding, born May 4, 1812, of whom more as Child 1.
3. Asbury Harding, born March 12, 1814; married to Mercy Ann Owens and had at least one son:

a. Zachariah Harding, born July 28, 1839, and of whom more in Chapter 6.

4. William Harding, born December 27, 1815
5. Daniel Harding, born April 7, 1818; predeceased his father, leaving children (not named in their grandfather's will).
6. Katherine Harding, born December 10, 1819; named Kitty Moore in her father's will. Reported in papers found in the family file at the Historical Society as married to Benjamin Moore. However, *Marriage Licenses, Montgomery County Maryland 1798-1898* by Janet Thompson Manuel reports that Catharine Harding (sic) was married in the county by license dated December 13, 1847 to Elias Moore, born c.1820 in Maryland. His full name could, of course, have included both Benjamin and Elias. He was head of household in the 1850 census of the Fifth District, listed as Elias, with his wife Catharine, and one child. Elias was next found as head of household in the 1860 census of the Fifth District, Sandy Spring Post Office, owner of $1,200 in real estate and $400 in personal property, with his wife and five children. They were listed next door to the household of his wife's parents. Elias was head of household in the 1870 census of the Fifth District, with Catharine, and four of their children. They were living next door to her brother Andrew Jackson Harding, and near other families with the surname Moore and Leizear, probably relatives. Elias was head of household in the 1880 census of the Fifth District, still listed next door to his wife's brother Andrew J. Harding. Elias was by then a widower, with one of his married sons in the household, and a niece and a nephew: Elizabeth A. Moore, born c.1866, and Charles W. Moore, born c.1871. Also in the household was Sarah F. Moore, born c.1842, a widow, listed as a sister-in-law; apparently the mother of the niece and nephew. The children of Elias and Catharine were:

a. Sarah Ann Moore, born c.1849, died February 20, 1930, survived by a daughter, Mrs. Robert J. T. Richardson, 7 grandchildren, 14 great grandchildren, and 2 great great grandchildren. She was married in the county by license dated May 9, 1865 to Jacob Van Horn, born c.1844 in Pennsylvania, died April 26, 1919 in Montgomery

County, Maryland. He was head of household in the 1870 census of the Fifth District, with his wife Sarah A., and two children. He was next found as head of household in the 1880 census of the Fifth District, with his wife and both daughters. He was head of household in the 1900 census of the Fifth District, with his wife, married thirty-two years, and she had been the mother of two children, only one of them then surviving. Living in the household was Walter Vanhorn, a nephew, born August, 1885 in New Jersey. Also living there was Elias Moore, the father-in-law. The children were:

(1) Martha E. Van Horn, born c.1867; apparently deceased before 1900.

(2) Alice V. Van Horn, born March 14, 1869, died June 15, 1957; buried at Colesville Methodist Church with her husband. Married by license dated February 26, 1889 in the county to Robert J. T. Richardson, born December 25, 1858, died December 17, 1939 at his home in Colesville. His Sentinel obituary names his wife, five daughters, two sons, a sister and a brother, and states that there were 21 grandchildren and 10 great grandchildren surviving. In transcribing the 1900 census, we read head of household #58 as being Robert R. Richardson, born December, 1861. His wife's name was recorded as Alice B., born March, 1860, but we are apparently there dealing with the same couple. They had been married eleven years, and she had been mother of four children, all living at home. Church records provide additional children:

    (a) Maude V. Richardson, born January, 1890, died shortly before March 17, 1960 at the Washington Sanitarium and Hospital. Census records and cemetery stone at Burtonsville Cemetery reported her name as Maude V. Richardson; the *Sentinel* announcement of her marriage reported Maude Elizabeth, apparently incorrectly. She was married January 30, 1907 at Colesville to Thomas Lee Lechlider, born

1886, died 1966, and they lived on Silver Spring Avenue in Silver Spring, Maryland. She was the mother of three daughters and two sons, and was survived by four sisters, two brothers, ten grandchildren and seven great grandchildren. The children were:

1. Mrs. Everette E. Schulze.
2. Mrs. William J. Wright.
3. Anna M. Lechlider, born c.1912, died c.1976; buried at Burtonsville Cemetery with her parents. Married Russell J. Stant.
4. Thomas L. Lechlider.
5. Francis D. Lechlider.

(b) Charles J. Richardson, born September, 1892

(c) Sarah Ethel Richardson, born August, 1895. Married a few days before September 20, 1918 at the Colesville Methodist Church to Guy P. Linkins, born c.1873, died c.1928; buried at the church cemetery.

(d) Florence A. Richardson, born March, 1898; married to Ray.

(e) Gladys J. Richardson, married August 4, 1928 in Rockville by the Baptist Church pastor to Percy C. Morris.

(f) R. Milton Richardson.

(g) Lula Roberta Richardson, born c.1901, died c.1974; buried at Burtonsville Cemetery. Married at the Rockville Methodist Church about January 11, 1924 to Leonard B. Edwards, born c.1899.

b. Mary E. Moore, born c.1851

c. Isaac J. Moore, born c.1853. In the 1880 census of the Fifth District, living at home with his widowed father, and with a wife Annie T., born c.1855.

d. Charles Moore, born c.1854

e. Ellen Moore, born c.1856; apparently the same child listed as Rebecca Moore in the 1870 census, perhaps a second given name.

7. Joseph Harding, born March 10, 1822, of whom more as Child 7.
8. Elizabeth Harding, born February 3, 1824, died February 17, 1892; and of whom more in Chapter 5.
9. Sarah Harding, born December 24, 1825.
10. Andrew Jackson Harding, born December 16, 1830, of whom more as Child 10.

CHILD 2

**Samuel R. Harding**
**1812-1881**

This son of John W. Harding (1789) and Sarah E. Moore (1788) was born May 4, 1812, died February 8, 1881. He was married to Emily Owens, born c.1818, and had children:

1. John Robert Harding, born August 29, 1839, died May 21, 1907. Married in Montgomery County by license dated March 16, 1863 to Martha Ann Brown. Martha was apparently the daughter of Robert Brown, born c.1790 in Ireland and head of household in the 1850 census of the Fifth District, with his wife and children, including Martha of the proper age. If we are correct, her mother would have been Fortunate M. Brown, born c.1806 and, according to the 1850 census, born "on the high seas." That is, she was born aboard ship while her parents were immigrating to America. John Robert Harding appeared as head of household in the 1900 census of the Fifth District of Howard County, Maryland, with his wife Martha, born c.1843, and two daughters:
    a. Sarah F. Harding, born c.1878
    b. Ada N. Harding, born c.1880
2. James W. Harding, born c.1844
3. Samuel Noah Harding, born December 13, 1844, died January 14, 1925. Married to Helen Augusta Iglehart, born August 25, 1846, died June 20, 1907. He was head of household in the 1900 census of the Fifth District of Howard County, with his wife and four children. There were other children:
    a. Samuel Herbert Harding, born January 19, 1873, died May 17, 1919. Married to Marian L. Boyle.

b. May Lydia Harding, born April 28, 1874, died October 10, 1949. Married to Walter Richardson.
c. Marshall Thomas Harding, born October 4, 1875, died December 13, 1956. In the 1900 census, he was listed as Thomas M. Harding, reversing his two given names. Married to Lula Batson Smallwood, born August 25, 1886, died August 24, 1964. Children:
   (1) Hazel Virginia Harding, born 1909, married Lester Young.
   (2) Marshall Thomas Harding, Jr., born September 15, 1913. Married to Thelma Rene Dudley, born September 29, 1921, died November 22, 1980. They had children:
      (a) Marsha Ann Harding, born December 22, 1953
      (b) Marshall Thomas Harding, III, born July 29, 1955
d. Caroline V. Harding, born October 19, 1877; married to William H. Harding. They appear to be the individuals of those names buried at Mt. Zion Cemetery at Highland, Maryland. William H. Harding is there indicated as born 1866 and died 1934.
e. Bentley Milton Harding, born May 17, 1880, died 1966. Married to Cora Burgess. In the 1900 census, his given names were reversed, reading Milton B. Harding. He is buried at the Mt. Zion Cemetery, indicated as born 1800, died 1966.
f. Mollie W. Harding, born June 5, 1883, died March 4, 1964. Married to Claude C. Cissel.
g. Lottie S. Harding, born August 20, 1885, died September 16, 1888.

4. Mary V. Harding, born c.1846, died January 15, 1920; married to William W. Iglehart. He may be the same as William Iglehart, born c.1842, a son of Isaac Iglehart (1800), who was head of household in the 1860 census of the Fifth District for the Sandy Spring Post Office area, with his wife and eight children, including William.
5. Sarah F. Harding, born c.1849, died c.1936. Married to George A. Scaggs.

CHILD 7

## Joseph Harding
## 1822-1894

This probable son of John W. Harding (1789) and Sarah E. Moore (1788) was born March 10, 1822 in Montgomery County, and died there April 26, 1894; buried in the Harding family cemetery near Cloverly, with his wife. Joseph was first married November 7, 1846 to Elizabeth J. Moore, born February 3, 1824, died December 27, 1853; buried in the Harding family cemetery. He was married second in the county by license dated February 11, 1869 to Josephine Geraldine Reynolds, born December 22, 1842, died May 15, 1915; buried with her husband. Also buried in the Harding family cemetery is Nathan Hosea Reynolds, born June 23, 1845, died December 16, 1929; perhaps a brother.

As a young man, Joseph bought a farm of about two hundred acres, being part of the tract called *Snowden's Manor Enlarged*, located at the intersection of the Colesville Turnpike and the Sandy Spring/Good Hope Road; then dirt lanes, but now the New Hampshire Avenue and Spencerville Road. Over the years, he developed an access road to the rear of the property, which has since become Harding Lane, where he built a three-story home for his growing family. For a time, he was toll-keeper on the Turnpike and was one of the founders of the Methodist Church near the village of Cloverly. Upon his death, the estate was divided between his children.

We first found Joseph as head of household in the 1850 census of the Fifth District, living next door to his parents, with the surname spelled Hardin in both cases. His wife Elizabeth was listed, with their first two children, Somerville and Mary V. Like his father, he was a farmer, although on a small scale, with only 30 acres of improved land and 70 acres unimproved, at $800 value. He owned 2 horses, 2 milch cows, and 16 swine. In the previous year he had produced 50 bushels of wheat, 150 bushels of Indian corn, 200 bushels of Irish potatoes and 100 pounds of butter.

Head of household in the 1860 census of the Fifth District of Montgomery County, Joseph Harding was born c.1822 in Maryland and was a farmer, listed with $3,800 in real estate and $1,000 in personal property. No female of an age to be his wife was found, but there appeared to be four children. Also living in the household was Mary Scott, born c.1807, a housekeeper; and James Cross, born c.1803, a black laborer. Head of household in the 1870 census of the Fifth District of Montgomery County, Joseph was listed with $10,000 in real estate and $2,450 in personal property. Josephine was listed with him in 1870, born c.1846, and there had been one child born to that marriage. Living in the household was Mary Scott, born c.1810, not identified. There were also four of his children born to his first marriage. He was next found as head of household in the 1880 census of the Fifth District of Montgomery County, listed adjacent to the household of his son Summerville Harding. His wife Josephine was there and they then had seven children at home. Mary Scott was still living with the family, indicated as married, and there were two black servants.

Joseph left a will in Montgomery County dated January 19, 1893, probated May 15, 1894, recorded in liber GCD 2 at folio 177, in which he names his wife, two daughters, his son Somerville, and the children of his deceased daughter Mary V. Cissell. Reference is made that they are children of his first wife. He makes specific bequests to that group of heirs, and then leaves the balance of his estate to his wife Josephine, "feeling assured that my children by her, my last wife, will be fairly and justly dealt with."

Josephine Harding was head of household in the 1900 census of the Fifth District, a widow, there reported as born December, 1848. She had been the mother of nine children, with eight surviving, and all at home. Living with her was a granddaughter, Sarah E. Cissel, born August 10, 1876. The children of Joseph Harding (1822) from his two marriages included:

1. Summerville Harding, born February 22, 1848, died June 16, 1931, and buried at Ivy Hill Cemetery, Laurel, Maryland. His given name was spelled Somerville in the 1870 census, perhaps more accurately. Married in the county by license dated March 31, 1869 to Susan Jane Tucker, born June 28, 1849, died April 5, 1924; buried with her husband. She was a daughter of Richard Tucker (1808), born in the District of Columbia, a carpenter, and Mary Amey or Amney (1815), born in Maryland. Susan Jane was living with her husband in

his father's household during the 1870 census. Summerville (sic) was head of household in the 1880 census of the Fifth District of Montgomery County, with his wife Susan, and three children. Also living in the household was Benjamin C. Tucker, born c.1852, listed as married, and a brother-in-law; and James H. Johnson, born c.1844, widower, farm laborer. Children were:

a. Edith May Harding, born May 14, 1870, died May 27, 1870
b. Ella Lee Harding, born April 14, 1871, died June 23, 1951. Married April 10, 1890 at Liberty Grove Methodist Church, Burtonsville, to William Howard Mullican, born c.1866, son of Barzilla Franklin Mullican (1833) and Jane Leadingham. They were not found in the 1900 census.
c. Idabel Harding, born October 31, 1873, died June 27, 1962; buried at Union Cemetery at Burtonsville with her husband. Married to John Robert Jones, born August 8, 1875, died December 22, 1937.
d. Clarice Virginia Harding, born July 12, 1876, died April 16, 1972; buried at the Masonic Home in Washington. Married to Frederick William Dierkoph.
e. Bertha Harding, a twin, born March 13, 1879, died July 8, 1879
f. Bessie Harding, a twin, born March 13, 1879, died July 13, 1879
g. Harvey Leon Harding, born February 7, 1881, and died April, 1963.
h. Lula Gertrude Harding, born May 3, 1884, died 1953; buried with her parents at Ivy Hill Cemetery, Laurel.
i. Goldie Stenna Harding, born October 8, 1886, died December 23, 1970 at the home of son Roland in Laurel. Married May 17, 1918 at Laurel to Samuel Edward Sweitzer, born April 6, 1886 at Laurel, died March 16, 1941, son of Samuel Sweitzer and Naomi Stanton. Children, born Fulton, Howard County:
   (1) Roland Beall Sweitzer, born July 10, 1919; married August 5, 1946 to Blanche Avis Wellford. They had children:

(a) Roland Beall Sweitzer, Jr., born November 25, 1950. Married October 10, 1970 Natalie Syfert and had at least one son:
    1. Jeffrey Scott Sweitzer: April 28, 1973
(b) Gregory Warren Sweitzer: October 3, 1960

(2) Ross Somerville Sweitzer, born October 13, 1922. Married July 17, 1946 to Virginia Bell Inscoe and had at least one daughter:
    (a) Debra Gail Bernadette Sweitzer, born July 4, 1951. Married c.1970 to Thomas Boxall, Jr.

2. Mary Virginia Harding, born January 12, 1850, died September 20, 1876; buried in the Harding family cemetery near Cloverly. Married to Clint Cissel and apparently had at least one daughter, living with her grandmother in 1900. Clint and Mary Virginia were not found in any census of the county. The children were:
    a. Sarah E. Cissel, born August 10, 1876, died January 16, 1911. Married to Wilford Baldwin.
    b. Florence V. Cissel.
3. Granville Harding, born August 2, 1851, died August 16, 1852; buried with his parents in the family cemetery near Cloverly.
4. Sarah Frances Harding, a twin, born July 15, 1853, died April 17, 1924. Married in the county by license dated May 30, 1872 to Hiram W. Hopkins, born May 8, 1849, died April 18, 1924; buried with his wife at Union Cemetery at Burtonsville. Notice the discussion following relative to the 1880 census, in which Hiram and his brother Samuel Jefferson were living in a double household. Head of household in the 1900 census of the Fifth District, Hiram was listed as a farmer, with Sarah F., married for twenty-eight years. She had been the mother of two children, both still at home:
    a. Mary E. Hopkins, born April, 1880
    b. Haywood Hopkins, born June, 1883
5. Elizabeth A. Harding, a twin, born July 15, 1853, died December 10, 1903. Married in the county by license dated June 10, 1872 to Samuel Jefferson Hopkins, born c.1847, a butcher. Samuel Jefferson Hopkins and his brother Hiram W. Hopkins, who married the twin Harding girls, were sons of

Samuel Hopkins (1823), a saddler and his wife Louisa E. Day (1824), who originally lived in the Cracklin District of the county. Louisa E. (Day) Hopkins died October 27, 1895, and was buried at Salem Cemetery, Brookeville. (*Sentinel* obituary). The 1880 census of the Fifth District is at best confusing in this area. The area was divided into two parts, one assigned to William F. Lazenby, and the other to J. S. Bohrer, Jr., both of whom enumerated the double household of the Hopkins brothers who had married the Harding twin girls. Mr. Lazenby reported the families as household #372, listing S. J. Hopkins as head of household in the 1880 census of the Fifth District, with his wife Lizzie A. and no children. He listed Hiram W. and his wife Sarah F., with one child. Samuel J. was head of household in the 1880 census of the Fifth District, with his wife, listed there as Lizzie A. of the proper age. They were living in a double household, with the other being headed by Hiram W. Hopkins, his brother, there reported with a wife named Sarah F., of the proper age. They then had Florence Cissel living with them, born c.1875, reported as a niece. Samuel J. and Elizabeth then did not have children. Mr. Bohrer enumerated many of the same households, overlapping the area assigned to Mr. Lazenby. Realizing his error, he then crossed through his enumeration sheets containing the households from 2-2 through 30-33, and again from 33-36 through 36-39. He had enumerated the double household 15-15 and 15-16, already reported by Mr. Lazenby. However, Mr. Bohrer reported Samuel J. Hopkins with a wife Sarah E., and Florence Cissel living with them; and Hiram W. Hopkins with a wife Lizzie A., and the child. He apparently had swapped the two girls with their husbands, but managed to get the daughter with the correct mother. It appears that Samuel J. and Elizabeth were the parents of:

a. Adella M. Hopkins, born May, 1880

6. Granville Harding, born August 2, 1851, and died August 16, 1852. buried in the Harding family cemetery near Cloverly.
7. Daughter Harding, born c.1870; one month old and unnamed at the time of the census taking.
8. Walter Joseph Harding, born June 18, 1871, died December 13, 1925; buried at Union Cemetery in Burtonsville with his

wife. Married June 18, 1902 at Liberty Grove Methodist Church, Burtonsville, to Annie Porter Thompson, born November 25, 1874, died June 10, 1954; the daughter of Benjamin F. Thompson (1835) and Amanda Flook. His *Sentinel* obituary states that he left a wife and an adopted child. He left a will in the county dated January 17, 1916, probated December 22, 1925, recorded in liber PEW 2 at folio 485, naming his wife Annie P.

9. Albert Alexander Harding, born August 10, 1872, died March 24, 1893. Buried in Harding family cemetery near Cloverly.
10. Blanche Emma Harding, born April 22, 1874, died January 31, 1915. Buried in Harding family cemetery near Cloverly.
11. Daniel Francis Harding, born August 22, 1875, died September 24, 1935. Buried in the Harding family cemetery near Cloverly.
12. Edith Viola Harding, born c.1877, died May 6, 1966 at Olney. Married September 28, 1912 at Liberty Grove Methodist Church, Burtonsville, to Louis Isaac Wrenn, born 1868, died 1936; buried with his wife at the Harding family cemetery near Cloverly.
13. Charles Lee Harding, born c.1879, died March 6, 1944 at the home of his sister, Mrs. Louis Isaac Wrenn. Buried in the Harding family cemetery near Cloverly, single.
14. Ernest Elmo Harding, born February 5, 1880, died December 20, 1934; buried in the Harding family cemetery near Cloverly. Married to Ella May Parks, born April 27, 1890, died October 9, 1938, daughter of George Washington Parks, and had children, the first two born at Baltimore, and the rest at Cloverly. He left a will dated December 24, 1934, probated February 13, 1935, recorded in liber HGC 5, at folio 493. It states that he was then of Rockville, but temporarily residing in Baltimore; and named only his wife. The children were:
    a. Marvel Louise Harding, born September 1, 1909; married December 20, 1936 to Clarence J. Andrae.
    b. Joseph Marion Harding, born August 19, 1917.
    c. Harold Ernest Harding, born December 20, 1924, died April 2, 1945 at the battle of Okinawa.
    d. Adrian Wesley Harding, born February 20, 1928.

e. Lois June Harding, born June 17, 1933; married April 21, 1951 to William Bryan Woodward.

15. Maude Irene Harding, born May 23, 1882, died August 1, 1933. Married April 13, 1903 to Harry Alonzo Turner, born June 8, 1878, died March 30, 1953; son of James Fletcher Turner (1850) and Mary Virginia Kemp (1844). Children:
    a. Eleanor Muriel Turner, born March 20, 1905; married June 17, 1931 to Hobert A. McCampbell.
    b. Kemp Reynolds Turner, born October 29, 1906; married September 19, 1929 to Ruth Mullings.
    c. Violet Audrey Turner, born August 24, 1908
    d. Harry Alonzo Turner, Jr., born January 11, 1912, died January 16, 1950. Married November 15, 1934 to Annie Emily Brigham, born October 15, 1917 at Redland in Montgomery County, and had children:
        (1) Harry Alonzo Turner, III, born February 1, 1942 in Washington; married March 4, 1967 Pegeen Willa Buice.
        (2) Walter Perry Turner, born at Olney February 23, 1945; married June 12, 1965 Linda Carol Jennings.
        (3) Mitchell Blair Thomas Turner, born February 24, 1953 at Bethesda.
    e. Stirling Carroll Turner, born January 5, 1914, married January 21, 1937 to his cousin, Edith Arlene Turner, born April 10, 1919, and had children:
        (1) Sylvia Yvonne Turner, born July 5, 1937 at Takoma Park, died June 9, 1971.
        (2) Carroll Wayne Turner, born at Olney April 17, 1940; married July 11, 1958 to Mary Ruth Leizear.
    f. Nathalie Frances Turner, born August 8, 1918, died July 25, 1965. Married June 2, 1940 to Woodrow Wilson Manuel.
    g. Colin Harding Turner, born June 4, 1920, married June 20, 1941 to Anne Stedman Moubray, born June 15, 1923 and had children:
        (1) Charles Colin Turner, born May 20, 1942 at Takoma Park. Married October 18, 1961 to Ellen Gertrude Lucas.
        (2) Bertie Anne Irene Turner, born April 1, 1946

h. Betty Jean Turner, born October 26, 1923; married May 29, 1945 to Joseph Lahocki.
i. Robert Lee Turner, born January 4, 1926; married April 9, 1960 to Joan Parson, born February 7, 1941 at Beartown, West Virginia, and had children, born at Takoma Park, Maryland:
    (1) Kathy Irene Turner, born May 26, 1961
    (2) Gary Lee Turner, born September 6, 1963
    (3) Larry Lee Turner, born January 8, 1965

16. Pearl Nathalie Harding, born May, 1884, died June 5, 1959 at Cloverly. Married October 30, 1911 to Archibald Stirling Turner of Norwood, born June 3, 1883, died April 3, 1951; son of James Fletcher Turner (1850) and Mary Virginia Kemp (1844). Archibald and Pearl are buried in the Harding family cemetery near Cloverly. At least two children:
    a. Edith Arlene Turner, born April 10, 1919; married January 21, 1937 to her cousin Stirling Carroll Turner, born January 5, 1914, and had children:
        (1) Sylvia Yvonne Turner, born July 5, 1937 at Takoma Park, died June 9, 1971.
        (2) Carroll Wayne Turner, born at Olney April 17, 1940; married July 11, 1958 to Mary Ruth Leizear.
    b. Alice Joyce Turner, born November 5, 1920; married July 26, 1939 at Colesville Methodist Church to Leonard Franklin Hobbs, born January 1, 1914, son of Claude Hobbs and Effie Riggs Ray (1887) of Layhill. Children:
        (1) Sandra Elaine Hobbs, born June 17, 1941, married June 15, 1962 William Robert O'Keefe and had at least two sons:
            (a) Dennis Robert O'Keefe: July 23, 1965
            (b) Curtis William O'Keefe: December 19, 1969.
        (2) Richard Eldon Hobbs, born July 18, 1947, married September 14, 1968 to Jo Ann Rohland of Four Corners, Maryland. At least two children:
            (1) Michael Richard Hobbs: September 9, 1970
            (2) Gary William Hobbs: October 24, 1973.

17. Ella May Harding, born 1890, died 1938; buried in the Harding family cemetery.

## CHILD 10

### **Andrew Jackson Harding**
### **1830-1907**

This son of John W. Harding (1789) and Sarah E. Moore (1788) was born December 16, 1830 in Montgomery County, Maryland, died December 21, 1907 and is buried at Cloverly, Maryland in the private Harding family lot near the school. Under the will of his father, he received two tracts of land, one known as *Estep*, containing ninety-eight and a half acres; and the other containing 105 acres; and also twelve or thirteen acres which he purchased from (illegible). In addition, he received "my two colored boys" George and Oliver, as well as the remainder of the personal estate of animals and household furniture. The condition of the bequest was that Andrew would continue to care for his mother during her natural life. Head of household in the 1870 census of the Fifth District of Montgomery County, listed only by his initials, A. J. Harding was born c.1831 in Maryland. He was a farmer, with $3,500 in real estate and $900 in personal property. He is probably Andrew J. Harding, married in the county by license dated November 21, 1865 to Maggie Myers; her full name was Margaret Elizabeth Myers, born August 12, 1844 in Frederick County, died April 8, 1882 (?). In the 1870 census, his wife is listed with him as Margaret, born c.1844, and there were two children. Living in the household was Samuel Johnson, born c.1850, a laborer.

A. J. Harding was next found as head of household in the 1880 census of the Fifth District of Montgomery County, with his wife Margaret, and seven children. Living in the household was Andrew J. Harding, born c.1849, a nephew. This younger Andrew was found in the 1870 census of the Fifth District with his surname spelled Hardin, a blacksmith apprentice, living in the household of Richard A. Burton (1845), a blacksmith.

Andrew J. Harding, the elder, was next found as head of household in the 1900 census of the Fifth District. However, his wife was there listed as Julia N., born May, 1855. The enumerator appears to have indicated here that Julia is a second wife of Andrew, which would appear correct based on the number of children she has had. However, *Marriage Licenses, Montgomery County Maryland 1798-1898* by Janet Thompson Manuel lists two marriages under the name of Andrew J. Harding, neither of them to this individual, and both apparently earlier. For the record, they were November 21, 1865 to Maggie Myers; and February 26, 1881 to Clara T. Richardson. In the 1900 census, it is reported that Andrew and Julia have been married seventeen years, and that she has been the mother of three children, only one surviving.

Andrew Jackson Harding left a will in Montgomery County, dated August 13, 1904, probated January 21, 1908, recorded in liber HCA 4 at folio 487. In the will, he named nine children. The children were:

1. Granville Jackson Harding, born October 18, 1867, died February 24, 1905; buried at Union Cemetery, Burtonsville. His obituary in the *Sentinel* stated that he left a widow and ten children. Married in Montgomery County by license dated November 7, 1887 to Katherine Williams, born July 16, 1863, died November 17, 1926; buried with her husband. He was head of household in the 1900 census of the Fifth District of Montgomery County, with his wife Kate, and nine children. They had been married fifteen years, and she had been the mother of nine children, all surviving, and at home. Children, all born at Cloverly, Maryland:
    a. Lawrence Edgar Harding, born January 30, 1886, died February 20, 1944; buried at Colesville Methodist Cemetery. Married on January 12, 1908 at the Lutheran Church in Baltimore to Carrie Belle Bowman, born July 10, 1888 at Brighton, Montgomery County, died 1977; buried with her husband. She was a daughter of Perry G. Bowman, born April 12, 1850, died February 24, 1921; and his wife Eva Elizabeth Basil, born September 22, 1856, died August 29, 1922; both of whom are buried at Friends Meeting House. Children, all born at Cloverly:
        (1) Bentley Leroy Harding, born July 6, 1910, obtained a marriage license in Washington about September, 1939 to marry Clara E. Rosal, born c.1910.
        (2) Gladys Irene Harding, born January 16, 1916; Liberty Grove Methodist Church, Burtonsville.

(3) Alice Lorraine Harding, born October 25, 1923 and married May 8, 1945 at the Colesville Methodist Church to Garnett DeWitt Inscoe, Jr. Children, born in Montgomery County, Maryland:
   (a) Lawrence Mead Inscoe: February 22, 1958
   (b) Rebecca Lee Inscoe: March 17, 1960
   (c) Donald Merrell Inscoe: March 25, 1966

b. Elsie Virginia Harding, born May 17, 1888, died July 16, 1968; buried at Union Cemetery, Burtonsville. Married Stewart G. Abell, born March 26, 1836, died July 11, 1956; buried at Friends Meeting House; and had four children:
   (1) Charles H. Abell.
   (2) Mildred Abell, married to Haugh.
   (3) John Robert Abell.
   (4) Mary K. Abell, married to Wainscott.

c. Herbert Lee Harding, born September, 1889, died c.1955; a carpenter. Buried at Union Cemetery at Burtonsville, where his stone indicates that he was a Maryland Wagoner, Co C, 307 Ammo Train, during the first world war. Served overseas May 19, 1918 to May 12, 1919. His wife was Myrtle M., born c.1896 in Baltimore, died May 30, 1988 at Montgomery General Hospital in Olney, and they had children, mentioned in their mother's obituary. There were also eight grandchildren, and ten great grandchildren. The children included:
   (1) Ruth Harding; married to Riggs of Kensington.
   (2) Louise Harding, married to Harry Marrow of Silver Spring, and had at least one child:
      (a) Milan H. Marrow, died before 1988.
   (3) Jean Harding, married to William Bready.
   (4) Gloria Lee Harding, married May 7, 1960 to Frank Valdenar, III.
   (5) Milan E. Harding.

d. Nettie Mae Harding, born July 24, 1891, died September 19, 1909. Married April 29, 1908 to James Ellis Bryan. Buried at Union Cemetery with her parents.

e. Lottie Charlotte Harding, born November 5, 1893, died July 11, 1958. Her stone in her father's plot at Union

Cemetery reads Charlotte Elizabeth Harding, with the proper dates.

f. Elizabeth B. Harding, born December 25, 1895, died June 10, 1902. Buried at Union Cemetery with parents.

g. Bertha Irene Harding, a twin, born May 10, 1896, died November, 1964. Married June 30, 1923 at Liberty Grove Methodist Church, Burtonsville, to Arthur C. Snyder, born c.1892.

h. Erman Granville Harding, a twin, born May 10, 1896, died April 29, 1984 at Washington Adventist Hospital in Takoma Park; buried Fort Lincoln Cemetery at Brentwood. Married January 25, 1928 to Lucy Jeanetta Burton of North Carolina. No children.

i. Horace Albert Harding, born July 7, 1898, died December 1, 1944.

j. Frank Myers Harding, born October, 1900, died July 26, 1973. Married to Mildred L.

k. Dallas Rayston Harding, born January 21, 1904, died July 8, 1919. Buried at Union Cemetery with parents.

2. James Henry Harding, born July 12, 1868, died June 21, 1942. Married in Montgomery County December 5, 1892 to Ada R. Moore, born July 14, 1873 at Spencerville, died April 27, 1913. Both buried at Union Cemetery, Burtonsville. Head of household in the 1900 census of the Fifth District, James H. and Ada had been married eight years, and she had then been the mother of two children, both at home. They had children, born at Spencerville:

a. Thomas James Harding, born September 25, 1892, died April 24, 1968 at Belmont Nursing Home; buried at Union Cemetery at Burtonsville with his wife. Married December 2, 1919 to Lillian Olivia Johnson, born September 30, 1894, died December 23, 1983 at Brooke Grove Nursing Home in Olney. They had one child:

(1) Carroll Wilson Harding, born August 22, 1923, and married May 28, 1953 to Betty Virginia Daugherty, born March 18, 1928 in Washington, daughter of Robert Daugherty and Bessie Raynes of Virginia; and had children:

(a) John Thomas Harding: April 14, 1954

(b) Carol Jane Harding: September 28, 1958
(c) Carroll Wilson Harding, Jr.: December 5, 1959
(d) James Lee Harding: December 17, 1963

b. Ethel Mae Harding, born August 26, 1894, died February 1, 1934. Married December 30, 1916 to Andrew Jackson Thompson, II and had three children.
c. Alton L. Harding, born August 24, 1905, died March 11, 1985 at Sharon Nursing Home in Olney; buried in Union Cemetery at Burtonsville. He served in the Coast Guard during the second world war, and was a retired Captain of Police in Montgomery County, having served in his final post as commander of the midnight shift at the Rockville Station. Married October 17, 1935 to Gladys Carlisle. Married second February 16, 1955 at Rockville to Louise Thompson, born February 14, 1908 in Rockville, died December 10, 2000 at the Wilson Health Care Center in Gaithersburg; buried at Union Cemetery in Burtonsville. She was the daughter of Samuel Walter Thompson (also found as Walter S. Thompson) and Bessie M. Belt, and had retired as a court clerk in Rockville. No children.
d. Russell Harding, born May 10, 1910, died August 11, 1910; buried with his parents.

3. Arthur Eugene Harding, born January 4, 1871, died May 2, 1953, and buried at Union Cemetery, Burtonsville. He was a builder in Montgomery County, and was married there by license dated December 23, 1896 to Susan Catherine Leizear, born December 23, 1879, died January 18, 1967 at Randolph Hill Nursing Home at Wheaton and buried with her husband. Susan was the daughter of William Perry Leizear and Ida J. Brown of Burtonsville. He was head of household in the 1900 census of the Fifth District, living alone with his wife Susie C., married for three years. Children, born at Cloverly:
   a. Eva Cornelia Harding, born March 29, 1902. Married December 31, 1940 to Clinton Franklin Wadford, and in 1984, was living in Clearwater, Florida.
   b. Mildred Irene Harding, born June 30, 1910, died August 22, 1910. Buried with her parents.

c. Stanley Arthur Harding, born October 19, 1911 at Cloverly, Maryland, died April 21, 1984 at Montgomery General Hospital in Olney; buried at Union Cemetery at Burtonsville. Married August 27, 1940 to Ruth Elizabeth Hawkins, born December 18, 1917 at Olney; daughter of Charles Robert Hawkins (1890) and Anna Elizabeth Story (1892). Stanley was a detective with the Montgomery County Police Department from 1941 to 1970, and was survived by his wife, two daughters, two sisters, a brother, and three grandchildren. His children were:
   (1) Delores Fay Harding, born November 12, 1942 at Olney, Montgomery County. Married July 21, 1968 to Carl Morris of Brookeville, and by 1984, lived in Dun Loring, Virginia.
   (2) Marlene Sue Harding, born November 28, 1948 at Olney, Maryland. Married to Breeding and lived in Silver Spring.

d. Elwood Lee Harding, born May 30, 1918 at Cloverly, Maryland. Married November 23, 1945 to Thelma Bowling, born November 26, 1919 in Charles County, a daughter of Frank Augustus Bowling and Ruth Lillian Penn. Staff sergeant, USA, second world war, enlisted from Rockville. Children, born in Washington, D. C.:
   (1) Barrett Lee Harding, born June 9, 1948
   (2) Steven Craig Harding, born March 3, 1950
   (3) Timothy Brian Harding, born May 14, 1959, died February 23, 1974 from accidental gunshot.

4. Harry Geisbert Harding, born August 24, 1874, died March 3, 1945. Married December 18, 1899 at Liberty Grove Methodist Church, Burtonsville, to Bertha Drucilla Leizear of Cloverly, born July 17, 1878, died July 3, 1963 at Fairland, the daughter of Joseph Leizear and Sarah C. Calvert. He was head of household in the 1900 census of the Fifth District of Montgomery County, listed as Henry G. Harding, living alone with his wife Bertha, in the first year of their marriage. They had children, the first two born at Cloverly and the rest at Fairland. Harry G. Harding left a will dated September 29, 1932 in Montgomery County, probated March 13, 1945, and

recorded in liber OWR 6 at folio 359, in which he bequeathed his entire estate to his wife Bertha. The children were:

a. Mabel Selina Harding, born March, 1901, died August 13, 1901.
b. Catherine Estelle Harding, born November 17, 1903; married October 10, 1929 at Liberty Grove Methodist Church, Burtonsville, to Clarence Edward Wright of Burtonsville. Her obituary states that she died December 26, 1987 at her home, and was buried at Union Cemetery at Burtonsville. Survived by her husband and a sister, there were apparently no children.
c. Harold Harry Harding, born April 18, 1908, died January 4, 1981 at Montgomery General Hospital; buried at Union Cemetery in Burtonsville; leaving six grandchildren and two great grandchildren. Married June 17, 1929 to Marion Elizabeth Roby, born March 7, 1905, the daughter of Edward Haslup Roby (1879) and Annie Emma Elizabeth Beckwith (1878). Children, born at Laurel, in Prince George's County:
    (1) Harold Alvin Harding, born March 15, 1930, and married July 11, 1953 at Liberty Grove Methodist Church, Burtonsville, to Shirlie Belle Walton of Greenbelt, Maryland, born April 10, 1933, and had children, born in Prince George's County:
        (a) Jacqueline Leigh Harding: March 13, 1954
        (b) Patricia Lynn Harding: March 8, 1956
    (2) Maurice Lee Harding, born June 17, 1935; married February 18, 1955 to Charlotte Roby Pritchard and had children, born at Laurel, Maryland:
        (a) Carol Ann Harding: January 26, 1956
        (b) Sandra Lee Harding: October 1, 1958
        (c) John Maurice Harding: December 21, 1959
        (d) Susan Marie Harding: February 9, 1964
d. Marion M'liss Harding, born November 30, 1912, and married March 20, 1934 to Russell Grove Rothgeb, born January 21, 1901. They had children:
    (1) Jean M'liss Rothgeb, born August 17, 1935; married August 25, 1962 to Miltides Aristotle Ganas and had children:

(a) Vic Ganas.
(b) Andrew Constantine Ganas.

(2) James Russell Rothgeb, born August 20, 1938; married March 26, 1960 to Virginia Lucille Carter.
(3) Donald Martin Rothgeb, born February 14, 1942; married November 25, 1966 to Betty Jane Camp and had children:
(a) Matthew Rothgeb.
(b) Julie Rothgeb.

5. John Randolph Harding, born December 5, 1876, died August 18, 1940; married to Mary. He is buried at Union Cemetery at Burtonsville in Montgomery County. He left a will in Montgomery County, dated 1938 (month and day illegible), which was probated September 10, 1940, recorded in liber HGC 33 at folio 229, listing the date of death. He leaves his entire estate to his wife, Mary D. Harding, for her natural life, and at her death, to be divided between Gertrude Neff and Nellie Montgomery, who are termed "her children" perhaps from an earlier marriage. The will states that he then owned a twenty-acre farm on the Beltsville Road in Montgomery County, which he divided in halves for the two girls by his will.
6. Edna Elizabeth Harding, born January 12, 1878, died March 30, 1959. Married September 29, 1897 at Liberty Grove Methodist Church, Burtonsville, to William O'Keefe, born June 3, 1871, died June 3, 1941; buried at Union Cemetery at Burtonsville. He was head of household in the 1900 census of the Fifth District with his wife Edna, married for two years, but with no children. They had children, born at Cloverly:
a. Gertrude Marie O'Keefe, born November 11, 1906. Married November 28, 1936 at Ellicott City to Wilbur Augustus Marth.
b. Granville Jackson O'Keefe, born July 23, 1908. Married March 14, 1936 to Mildred Elizabeth Ricketts.
c. Douglas William O'Keefe, born July 24, 1912. Married August 24, 1940 to Sarah Bryant.
d. Russell Harding O'Keefe, born February 17, 1914. Married April 14, 1945 to Dorothy Lee Van Horn.
e. Bernice Elizabeth O'Keefe, born December 21, 1917. Married December 8, 1945 to Gerald Chester Mollock.

7. William Franklin Harding, born April 5, 1880, October 22, 1948; buried at Colesville Methodist Church. Married to Virginia Culver, born 1883, died 1961; buried with her husband. She was a daughter of George H. Culver (1854). William F. left a will in the county dated May 5, 1945, probated November 17, 1948, recorded in liber WCC 13 at folio 2, leaving everything he possessed to his wife and named her Executor of his estate. No mention of children.
8. Margaret Rebecca Harding, born April 10, 1882, and died June 13, 1961; buried in the Union Cemetery at Burtonsville. Married October 10, 1905 to William Edward Johnson, born February 12, 1873, died February 26, 1973; buried at Union Cemetery at Burtonsville with his wife and one daughter. Margaret's obituary states that they lived near Spencerville, and that she was a "member of a distinguished Maryland family." Survived by three daughters and a son:
    a. Alice May Johnson, born March 26, 1906, died July 11, 1908; buried with her parents.
    b. Dorothy Johnson, married to Wootton.
    c. Eleanor Johnson, married to Patton.
    d. Gladys Johnson, married to Patton.
    e. Robert Johnson.
9. Lewis Montgomery Harding, born August 15, 1890, died December, 1961; apparently the only child of Julia who survived. Married to Annie Gertrude and had at least one son:
    a. Harvey Harding.

# CHAPTER 5

## Elizabeth Harding
## 1824-1892

This daughter of John W. Harding (1789) and Sarah E. Moore (1788) was born February 3, 1824 in Montgomery County, Maryland, and died there February 17, 1892. In her father's will she was referred to as Elizabeth Wilson. Married December 19, 1848 to William Franklin Wilson, born January 30, 1817 in Montgomery County, died May 9, 1901, the son of John Wilson. He had been previously married to Keys, by whom he had at least one child. He appears to be the same William Wilson found as head of household in the 1860 census of the Fifth District, Sandy Spring Post Office. He was there reported as born c.1817, a farmer, owning $3,000 in real estate and $1,500 in personal property. His wife Elizabeth was reported there as born c.1823, and they then had six children. In the 1870 census of the Fifth District, he was listed as William F. Wilson, head of household, with his wife Elizabeth, and nine children. He then owned $4,000 in real estate and $1,500 in personal property. William F. Wilson was next head of household in the 1880 census of the Fifth District, with the surname spelled Willson, rather than Wilson. His wife Elizabeth was there, with five children still at home. The children were:

1. William Adolphus Wilson, born October 8, 1849. Listed only as William Wilson in the 1860 census, appeared as Adolphus in the 1870 census. Married to Laura Cole.
2. Sarah Elizabeth Wilson, born May 17, 1851, died c.1930; still at home in 1880. Married to John F. Link, born March 29, 1865 in Howard County, Maryland; died August 6, 1950.
3. Mary Catherine Wilson, born February 1, 1853. Married Horace Wilson, born c.1850.
4. John Henry Wilson, born February 22, 1855 at Ednor, died June 10, 1923 at Fulton, Maryland. Married March 1, 1882 to Martha Letitia Browning, born December 20, 1859 in Howard County, died June 28, 1935 at Burtonsville, Montgomery County, daughter of William Browning and Ellen Lawrence. Children, the first born at Ednor, and the rest at Fulton:

a. Elsie L. Wilson, born October 20, 1884; married June 10, 1906 to Harry S. Wheeler and had children:
   (1) Lawrence Stanley Wheeler, married to Catherine A. Gibson.
   (2) William Russell Wheeler, married to Eleanor Mae Gibson.
   (3) Hazel Wheeler, married to Salter.
   (4) Tyson Wheeler.
   (5) Elmer D. Wheeler.
   (5) Harry Melvin Wheeler.
b. Corrie Elizabeth Wilson, born January 28, 1886; married April 19, 1909 to Ernest Harper.
c. William Henry Wilson, born July 8, 1887 at Fulton, died November 11, 1957 in Washington. Married May 28, 1901 in Ellicott City, Maryland Mary Gertrude Marlow, born April 12, 1891 at Ashton, Maryland, died December 22, 1972. At least one child:
   (1) William Leslie Wilson, married Viola Lindsay and had children:
      (a) Juanita Wilson.
      (b) Donald Wilson.
      (c) John W. Wilson.
d. Roy Haywood Wilson, born October 30, 1890, died May 11, 1936 at Burtonsville. Married to Carrie Frank Roby, born January 1, 1885 at Fairland, died there July 3, 1975. They had children, probably all born at Fairland:
   (1) Letitia May Wilson, married to Norman Oldham Garner.
   (2) Roy Lee Wilson.
   (3) Thelma Elizabeth Wilson, married to Carl LeRoy Kruhm.
   (4) Mildred Audrey Wilson, born November 7, 1917, died February 13, 1924.
   (5) Talmadge Duane Wilson.
   (6) Donald Roby Wilson.
   (7) Audrey Genevieve Wilson, married to Ernest Finnance and had children:
      (a) Martin Barnard Finnance.

(b) Letitia Marie Finnance, married to Randall Herman Canal.

e. Norman Leslie Wilson, born September 24, 1892.

5. Franklin Littleton Wilson, born March 1, 1857, died June 26, 1923. Married to Anna Amelia Jamison, born February 22, 1857, died September 13, 1941, the daughter of Uzziel Wakefield Jamison and Margaret Hall Spence. Children, born in Montgomery County:
   a. Anna Elizabeth Wilson, born c.1879, died March 26, 1967. Married October 19, 1898 to Edgar Parsley, born c.1875, died c.1964
   b. Margaret Claretta Wilson, born c.1881, died c.1965. Married September 25, 1911 to Richard T. Carr, born c.1883, died c.1929.
   c. Frank Hallowell Wilson, born March 14, 1889, of whom more following.
6. Silas Randolph Wilson, born October 19, 1859, died c.1865.
7. Margaret Ella Wilson, born January 1, 1862; married Charles Tippett Disney.
8. Laura Frances Wilson, born March 7, 1864, died April 3, 1929. Married c.1894 to Edward H. Carr.
9. Cyrus Seymour Wilson, born July 15, 1868, died c.1961 at Spencerville. Married in the county by license dated December 15, 1891 to Mary Ann Carr, born c.1872, died c.1951. Cyrus S. Willson (sic) was head of household in the 1900 census of the Fifth District, with wife Mary A., born June, 1872; married for eight years. She had been the mother of three children, all living at home. Living with them was William F. Willson (sic), at the age of 83 years, listed as father, and retired. The children were:
   a. Virgie May Wilson, born May 13, 1893; married December 27, 1917 at Ednor to Wilmer Rich.
   b. Edward Seymour Wilson, born May 16, 1895
   c. Caleb Lawrence Wilson, born January 21, 1897
   d. Lottie Marie Wilson, born c.1900; married Doctor Harry Upshall.
   e. Grace Kathryn Wilson, born c.1903, died c.1944; married to Hughes.
   f. Lee Jennings Wilson.

g. Kenneth Wilson.
h. John Woodrow Wilson; married Mary Gladys Hall.
i. Raphael Wilson, died June 12, 1911.

10. Sophie M. Wilson, born c.1870; an infant death.

## Frank Hallowell Wilson
## 1889-1964

This son of Franklin Littleton Wilson (1857) and Anna Amelia Jamison (1857) was born March 14, 1889 in Montgomery County, and died June 2, 1964 in Carroll County, Maryland. Married c.1918 to Edna Mae Boring, born January 21, 1897 at Baltimore, died July 2, 1967; daughter of George Washington Boring and Mary Virginia Wilhelm. They had children, at least some of them born at Burtonsville, Montgomery County:

1. Elva Virginia Wilson, married Albert Woodrow Thompson and had children:
    a. Dale Thompson, married Jan Miller; at least a daughter:
        (1) Elizabeth Miller Thompson.
    b. Duane Elton Thompson, married Mary Ann Macauley and had children:
        (1) Duane Elton Thompson, Jr.
        (2) Emily Thompson.
2. Dellora Mae Wilson, married three times: Charles Loan; John Gall; and Alfred Smeltzer. She had children:
    a. Carolyn Loan, married Donald Davis and second to Thomas Beatty. Children:
        (1) Mark Frederick Beatty, married Diane; children:
            (a) Daniell Beatty.
            (b) Bethany Beatty.
    b. Bonny Gall, married Jerry Norton and had children:
        (1) Kelly Norton, married Billy Lepper and had a child:
            (a) Jessica Lepper.
        (2) Jerry Norton, Jr., married Rebecca; children:
            (a) Jack Norton.
            (b) Cody Norton.
            (c) Luke Norton.
        (3) Heather Norton, married Brian Allen. Children:
            (a) Brianna Allen.

(b) Zachary Allen.

c. Margaret Gall, married twice; second to Gene Storms and had a child:

(1) Erik Storms.

3. Frank William Wilson, married three times; first to Carolyn Kasaah. At least one son:

a. Frank Benjamin Wilson.

4. Anna Elizabeth Wilson, born August 2, 1921, died December 15, 1985. Married to Francis Clay Kennedy. Children:

a. Patricia Lynn Kennedy, married David Lee Berry and had children:

(1) Rhiannon Leigh Berry.

(2) Holly Elizabeth Berry.

b. Sandra Elizabeth Kennedy, married Gordon Lee Davis, Jr. and had children. Married second John Robert Buckler, born 1948, died 1998; and third Gary Ray Saville. The children were:

(1) Kimberly Beth Davis, married first to Michael Darrin Vitt and second to Tony Saville. Children:

(a) Taylor Elizabeth Vitt.

(2) Misti Lee Davis, married to Bruce Alan Zimmerman and had children:

(a) Garrett Alan Zimmerman.

(b) Noelle Lee Zimmerman.

(3) Heather Anne Davis, married Erik Christian Helm.

(4) Kirk Gordon Davis.

(5) Sean Kennedy Davis.

(6) Ryan Patrick Davis.

(7) Chantal Nicole Davis.

(8) Sarah Elizabeth Saville.

(9) Daniel Lynn Saville.

(10) Richard William Saville.

c. Nancy Clay Kennedy, married Howard Lee Spencer and had a child:

(1) Howard Lee Spencer, Jr., married Melissa Ann Canipe and had a son:

(a) Howard Lee Spencer, III.

# CHAPTER 6

## Zachariah Harding
## 1839-1911

This son of Asbury Harding (1814) and Mercy Ann Owens was born July 28, 1939, and died February 14, 1911 at his home near Cedar Grove, in Montgomery County, Maryland, leaving his wife, four sons and a daughter. He is apparently the same found as Zachariah Hardin, of the proper birth year, head of household in the 1900 census of the Fifth District with a wife, Caroline V., born November, 1839. Married for thirty-eight years, she had been the mother of seven children, five surviving, and two grandchildren living at home. They were William L. Harding, born April, 1890; and Rubie Harding, born February, 1896.

The only son of this family that we can identify with certainty is Zachariah Harding, Jr., born c.1867, which accounts for only one of the five children still living in 1900. Although it is not an acceptable practice for genealogists, we wish here to discuss some of the possible other children. In the 1900 census of the Second District, Zachariah was living in a double household; that is, more than one family group in a single dwelling. The other family listed was that of James A. Baker, born June, 1874. He was married in the county by license dated December 18, 1897 to Ida V. (or Addie V.) Harding, born June, 1879. We suggest that she was one of the daughters of Zachariah and his wife Caroline.

Next door to the double household, we found a household headed by John E. Hardin (sic), born November, 1863. We suggest that he is also a child of Zachariah and Caroline. He was married to Annie M. King, born May, 1869.

About twelve households away, we found Nicholas Hardin (sic), born November, 1872, living in the household of John D. Burdette (1875). John D. Burdette was married to Maggie M. King (1877), who was a sister of Annie M. King (above), both girls being daughters of Charles C. King (1846). We suggest that Nicholas is yet another child of Zachariah and Caroline. If we are correct in these assumptions, the children would have been:

1. John E. Harding, born November, 1863. Married in the county December 12, 1894 to Hannah M. King (1869), daughter of Charles C. King (1846) and Mary E. Watkins (1847). She is also reported as Anna Mary (King) Harding, born c.1870, died October 8, 1926 at her home near Darnestown; leaving her husband, two daughters and six sons. With his surname read as Hardin from the census, he was head of household in the 1900 census of the Second District, living next door to Zachariah Harding (who is his father if we are correct in our analysis), with his wife Annie M. They had been married for six years, and she had been the mother of three children, all surviving. There was a fourth child in the household, apparently from an earlier marriage of John. His first wife was apparently Ida L., born c.1865, died June 5, 1892; wife of John E. Harding; buried at Neelsville Presbyterian Cemetery. The four children at home were:
    a. John Robert Harding, born March, 1887. Inducted September, 1917 at Rockville as private, 328th Regiment, Co E. He received a shell wound in leg and thigh, October 10, 1918. Discharged May 28, 1919.
    b. Katie M. Harding, born November, 1895
    c. Charles Harding, born August, 1897
    d. Eddie B. Harding, born February, 1899
2. Zachariah Harding, Jr., born c.1867, of whom more.
3. Nicholas Harding, born November, 1872. Married by license dated June 1, 1893 at Rockville to Mary C. Sherrer; filed suit for divorce December 1, 1911. Perhaps the same of that name born November 5, 1872, died June 22, 1957, buried at Forest Oak Cemetery in Gaithersburg. Buried with him is Annie V., noted as his wife, born May 12, 1875, perhaps a second marriage following the divorce. In the 1900 census of the Second District, we found Nicholas Harding, born November, 1872, but listed as single, living in the household of John D. Burdette (1875). In that report the surname was interpreted as Hardin.
4. Addie V. Harding, born June, 1879. married in the county by license dated December 18, 1897 to James A. Baker, born June, 1874. Head of household in the 1900 census of the Second District of Montgomery County, James was living with

his wife and one child in the same dwelling unit as Zachariah Harding, born 1839. James was born June, 1874 in Pennsylvania; his wife Addie V. (or Ida V.) was born June, 1879 in Maryland, and they had been married two years, parents of two children, both living, but only one at home. There were other children, born after the census, reported in records of Potomac Methodist Church, including:

a. William Edward Baker, born July 25, 1899 at Germantown, baptized at age 12 on October 29, 1911 at Potomac Methodist Church, died at Germantown June 30, 1985; buried at Forest Oak Cemetery in Gaithersburg. He was survived by his wife, four sons, seven daughters, thirty-eight grandchildren and twenty-five great grandchildren. One son, Edward L. Baker, predeceased him in 1980. Married January 19, 1921 at Grace Church in Gaithersburg, to Eleanor V. Howard, daughter of Linwood Howard (1874) and Florence Small of Quince Orchard. Eleanor was born c.1905 and died October 5, 1994. The children, not necessarily in birth order, were:
    (1) William L. Baker, born c.1926, died November 15, 1980 at Montgomery General Hospital in Olney; buried at Laytonsville Cemetery. He was the retired maintenance foreman for the Park and Planning Commission and had served in the second World War, receiving the Purple Heart. Survived by his wife, Lois Fraley, a daughter and two sons, as well as two grandsons. His obituary also names seven sisters and four brothers. Places of residence are as of 1980. Lois Fraley Baker was born c.1930, died June 13, 1993 at Montgomery General Hospital, and is buried with her husband. Her obituary names a total of four grandchildren. The children were:
        (a) Grace Elaine Baker, of Laytonsville; married to Gregory after 1980.
        (b) George E. Baker, of Gaithersburg; married with children:
            1. George E. Baker, Jr.
            2. Thomas W. Baker.
            3. Justina M. Baker.

(c) David L. Baker, of Laytonsville. Married and had a child:
    1. Ashley M. Baker.
(2) Virginia Baker, married to Blair, of Gaithersburg.
(3) Martha Baker, married to Wynkoop of Frederick.
(4) Marcella Baker, married to Kunzle of Florida.
(5) Alice Baker, married to Thompson of Wheaton.
(6) Anna Baker, married to Crowley of Thurmont.
(7) Dorothy Baker of Florida.
(8) Shirley Baker, married to Duley of Middletown.
(9) Howard Baker, of Florida.
(10) James Baker, of Gaithersburg.
(11) Robert Baker, of Pennsylvania.
(12) Douglas Baker, of Germantown.

b. Carrie Virginia Baker, born c.1901, baptized at the age of ten years on October 29, 1911.
c. Della May Baker, born c.1903; baptized at the age of eight years on October 29, 1911.
d. Mamie Gertrude Baker, born c.1906; baptized at the age of five years on October 29, 1911 at Potomac Methodist Church.

## Zachariah Harding, Jr.
## 1867-1923

This son of Zachariah Harding (1839) was born c.1867 in Montgomery County, and died April 7, 1923 at the home of his son in Washington, D. C.; buried at Forest Oak Cemetery. He was twice married; first to Grace Hodson, born c.1873, died May 2, 1900 at the age of twenty-seven years, one month and four days, buried at Forest Oak Cemetery. They had children, four of whom survived their father. Married second February 27, 1901 to Marie Belle Thompson of Travilah, from which marriage five children survived. His children were:

1. Elmer Lee Harding, born February 8, 1892, died December 20, 1947; buried at Forest Oak in Gaithersburg. Married January 10, 1912 at the Methodist Church in Gaithersburg to Grace C. Mullican; both bride and groom being of Gaithersburg. Grace was born c.1897, died February 8, 1980 at the

Wilson Health Care Center in Gaithersburg; buried at Forest Oak Cemetery. She was a daughter of Sarah F. (Mullican) Walker, who died July 14, 1937 in Gaithersburg. The obituary of Grace mentions a sister, Mamie Harding of Silver Spring, that her husband predeceased her and that she was survived by three children:

a. Frances Harding, married to McBrian of Silver Spring.
b. Dorothy L. Harding, married to Williams of Port Republic, Maryland.
c. Merle Harding, of Silver Spring.

2. Robert Donald Harding, born October 14, 1891, died November 29, 1961; buried at Forest Oak, Gaithersburg. Grave reported not marked. He was perhaps the husband of Bessie T. Bowman, born c.1923 in Virginia, died June 10, 1988 at Holy Cross Hospital in Silver Spring; buried at Parklawn Cemetery. She was a daughter of John and Thelma Bowman, and the mother of:
   a. Buddy E. Harding, named in the obituary of his brother Donald.
   b. Donald D. Harding, born July 2, 1945 in Sandy Spring, died October 3, 1988 at Shady Grove Hospital; buried at Parklawn Cemetery at Rockville. He was survived by a daughter:
      (1) Melissa Harding, of Frederick.
   c. Pepsi Harding, married to Ecker.
3. Carroll B. Harding, born c.1895, died c.1966; buried at Forest Oak Cemetery, Gaithersburg. Married to Mamie Mullican; a daughter of Sarah F. (Mullican) Walker, who died July 14, 1937 in Gaithersburg. It should be noted that this Walker family is not related to those commonly found in Montgomery County, but have their origins in Kansas.
4. Raymond Whitney Harding; infant baptism July 27, 1900. Born December 17, 1899, died December 6, 1971. Served as Chief Carpenter, USN, second world war. Wife Dorothea Runyan, born July 15, 1897. Damascus Methodist Church Cemetery.
5. Brawner Zachariah Harding, died suddenly March 25, 1979 at Frederick Memorial Hospital. He was married in Rockville July 2, 1925 by the pastor of the Christian Church to Marie

Frances Briggs, both bride and groom being of Gaithersburg. She was born March 8, 1908, died January 21, 1995; a daughter of Samuel Benjamin Briggs (1879) and Lelia G. Heim (1886); They had children, born in Gaithersburg, and at the time of her death, eleven grandchildren and five great grandchildren. Known as B. Z. to a large circle of friends and admirers, he was active in the Democratic party, and for several years, a welcome neighbor of the author, living on Montgomery Avenue in Gaithersburg. The children were:

a. Anna Marie Harding, born November 19, 1927; married first to Charles Stiles and second to William Perrell.

b. Barbara Jeanette Harding, born November 9, 1933; married August 27, 1955 to Charles Thomas White, born March 13, 1933, baptized October 21, 1934. He was a son of Washington Waters White, Jr. (1903) and Louisa Hood Griffith (1903). Charles has been Mayor of the town of Laytonsville for a number of years. Children, born in Montgomery County:

(1) Carol Marie White, born June 4, 1958. Married June 17, 1989 Michael Kamp, and had a daughter:

(a) Jenna Marie Kamp, born January 30, 1992

(2) Deborah Griffith White, born March 22, 1960. Married July 20, 1985 to Barry Bennett. Children:

(a) Bradley Wayne Bennett, born October 2, 1989

(b) Cory Thomas Bennett, born March 21, 1994

(c) Dylan White Bennett,born March 18, 1996

(3) Julia Briggs White, born May 21, 1962.

(4) Mary Louisa White, born May 14, 1966. Married December 15, 1990 at the Damascus Methodist Church to Kevin Wayne Helmick. A son:

(a) Kyle Wayne Helmick, born January 5, 1994.

c. Gloria Harding, born July 28, 1937; married to Norman Howard.

d. Robert Brawner Harding, born January 10, 1940; married to Nancy Riggs.

6. Paul D. Harding; apparently married with at least one son:

a. Paul D. Harding, Jr.; T/5, USA, second world war from Kensington.

7. Mary McLean Harding; married to Fenwick, of Silver Spring.

8. Francis B. Harding, born c.1910, died May 23, 2000 at Shady Grove Adventist Hospital near Gaithersburg. From 1949 to 1983, he owned and operated the F. B. Harding Electrical Construction Co.; served in the Navy in the Pacific during the second world war, and was a member of Grace Methodist Church and the Congressional Country Club. His first wife, Helen M. Harding, died in 1973, and he was survived by his second wife, Eloise T. Harding of Gaithersburg, ten grandchildren, fifteen great grandchildren, and children:
   a. Helen J. Harding, married to Barry.
   b. Francis B. Harding, Jr.
   c. Lorraine E. Harding, a stepdaughter.
   d. Paul M. Barth, a stepson.
9. Martha C. Harding; married to Grubb and lived in Newport News, Virginia.

# CHAPTER 7

## Elias Harding
## Died c.1832

It is possible that this Elias Harding was married in Frederick County by license dated January 9, 1786 to Cassandra Ford, the daughter of John Ford (1720) and Ruhama Howard. We note that one of his daughters was named Cassandra F. Harding, perhaps for her mother. Elias Harding died about 1832, intestate, and the heirs, his children, were determined on June 23, 1832. See Montgomery County deeds, liber BS 4, folio 29. The property was the home farm known as *Wayman's Purchase*, containing 130 acres, and a tract of 110 acres in Frederick County where James Powers and Elisha Trail were then living. On September 5, 1836, the property was awarded to William Bennett and Lloyd F. Harding. The children appeared to be:

1. Rebecca R. Harding, married in the county by license dated January 8, 1810 to Edward W. Gatton.
2. Cassandra F. Harding, married in Frederick County by license dated June 16, 1825 to James Powers. They were not found in the 1850 census of Frederick County.
3. Elizabeth Harding, married to Stanislaus Knott, born c.1793, and of whom more.
4. Lloyd F. Harding, born c.1794, of whom more.
5. Emaline Harding, reportedly married to Elias H. Hartsock and had at least three children, although we did not find the name in a Montgomery County census:
    a. Cassandra Hartsock.
    b. John Hartsock.
    c. Hilleary Hartsock.
6. Eleanor F. Harding, predeceased her father.
7. David Harding, perhaps (may have been husband of Eleanor rather than a sibling).
8. Charles F. Harding, predeceased his father, leaving three children as heirs.
9. John H. Harding.

## Elizabeth Harding

This daughter of Elias Harding (d/1832) was born in Montgomery County, and married there to Stanislaus Knott. He was born c.1793, son of Zachariah Knott (1741), who died November 23, 1820 and is buried at St. Mary's Cemetery, Barnesville. Stanislaus' sister, Mary Ann, was married as his first wife to Lloyd F. Harding, brother of Elizabeth.

Zachariah Knott was born in what was then Prince George's County about 1741, a son of William Knott. In 1748, soon after his birth, the area became part of Frederick County, and in 1776, finally part of present-day Montgomery. William left a will in the county dated July 25, 1795, probated April 7, 1802, recorded in liber D at folio 547, rerecorded in book VMB 1 at page 494. He named his wife Mary, and left to his son William Knott part of the tract called *Conclusion*. Part of the same tract was left to his son Thomas, and the tract called *Fox Race Ground* on which the home dwelling was located, was left to his son Philip. The will mentions two other sons, Zachariah and Henry. Two daughters; Jane and Mary; received the sixty-eight acre tract due their father from Colonel Francis Deakins.

Zachariah Knott left his will in Montgomery County, dated February 11, 1820, probated December 12, 1820, recorded in liber M at folio 281; rerecorded in book VMB 3 at page 115. To his son Stanislaus, he left one-half of the lands on the north side of the road from the Mouth of Monocacy to Ellicott's Mills. To daughter Teresa Knott (Jones), he left the other half of that tract of land. To his wife Jane, he left the home plantation, plus forty acres purchased from John Belt; all of it at her death to be divided between Stanislaus, his brother Joseph, and their sister Mary Ann (who was married to Lloyd F. Harding). The will mentioned several other family members as well.

Stanislaus Knott is apparently the same of that name found as head of household in the 1850 census of the Third District, born c.1793, and perhaps a widower, with six children at home. Stanislaus Knott was married second in the county by license dated September 28, 1850 to Bridgett Graham, born c.1827 in Ireland. He next appeared as head of household in the 1860 census of the Third District, with his second wife Bridgett, and four children, all born to that marriage. None of the children born to Elizabeth Harding were present, nor were they found anywhere else in the 1860 census. Stanislaus left a will in the county, dated April 15, 1862, probated January 11, 1865, recorded in liber JWS 1 at folio 172, leaving bequests to his wife Bridget and the four children born to their marriage. His children included:

1. Cassandra J. Knott, born c.1831
2. Peter C. Knott, born c.1833
3. John Elisha Knott, born June 8, 1833, died June 16, 1904; buried at St. Mary's in Barnesville, with his wife. Married to Mary Frances Clagett, born March 3, 1838, died March 2, 1900. Buried with them is one infant daughter. John Elisha Knott was married secondly in July, 1901 to Alice F. Cooley, daughter of John F. Cooley. There is no record of children.
4. Trecy Eleanor Knott, born c.1837
5. Ann Rebecca Knott, born c.1839
6. Mary C. Knott, born c.1841
7. Zachariah M. Knott, born c.1852, died 1933. He and the next three children are not in the blood lineage of the Harding families, but are half-brothers and sisters to the six children born to Stanislaus Knott and Elizabeth Harding.
8. James Edward Knott, born c.1853, died 1931.
9. Mary Jane Knott, born c.1854, died 1935.
10. Margaret Ann Knott, born June 6, 1859, died January 6, 1916 in Washington. Married in the county by license dated April 10, 1882 to Alexander F. Jamison, born March 13, 1852, died August 13, 1909; buried at St. Mary's Catholic Church in Barnesville with his wife. He was the son of Alexander F. Jamison (1804), and Theresa Harding (1827), who were listed in the 1880 census of the Medley District, with five children, including Alexander. Her obituary states that they had four children. He was head of household in the 1900 census of the Eleventh District, with his wife Anna, married for nineteen years. She had been the mother of five children, four surviving and living at home:
    a. Roger Edward Jamison, born November 2, 1884.
    b. Mary Lillian Jamison, born January 24, 1889
    c. Leo Knott Jamison, born September 9, 1892
    d. Dorothy Elizabeth Jamison, born April 28, 1895

## Lloyd F. Harding
## 1794-1861

This son of Elias Harding (d/1832) was born c.1794 in Montgomery County, Maryland, and died about December, 1861. He was head of household in the 1850 census of the Third District of Montgomery County, born c.1794 in Maryland, and was a farmer, listed with $3,000 in real estate. His wife was Sophia, born c.1794 in Maryland, and they then had three children living at home, all born in Maryland. Lloyd was apparently married twice; first in the county by license dated September 5, 1825 to Mary Ann Knott, and second by license dated November 27, 1830 to Sophia M. Hall. At the time of the 1850 census, Lloyd F. Harding was the owner of four slaves. He was next found as head of household in the 1860 census of the Third District, owning $2,850 in real estate and $899 in personal property. His wife Sophie M. was still at home, with the same three children found in the 1850 census.

Lloyd F. Harding left a will in the county dated June 9, 1856, probated December 3, 1861, recorded in liber JWS 1 at folio 96, in which he confirms to his daughter Theresa Jamison for her natural life, and at her death, to her children, everything he has already given to her, or made available to her during his lifetime. In addition, she is to receive one-fourth of his estate remaining after that bequest is taken out of the total. He then leaves the remainder to his wife Sophia for her natural life, and at her death to be divided equally between the three children of their marriage, and names them. Children included:

1. Theresa Harding, born June 29, 1827 to her father's first marriage; baptized July 8, 1827 at St. John's Catholic Church at Forest Glen, died c.1909. Married in the county by license dated September 6, 1844 to Alexander F. Jamison, born c.1804, died c.1890; buried at St. Mary's Cemetery in Barnesville, with his wife and several children. He was listed as Alex and head of household in the 1880 census of the Medley District, born c.1815, with his wife, there listed as Trisa, of the proper age. They then had five children at home. There were others:
   a. Lloyd I. Jamison, born c.1845, died c.1878; buried with his parents.

b. Alexander F. Jamison, born March 13, 1852, died August 13, 1909; buried at St. Mary's cemetery in Rockville. Married in the county by license dated April 10, 1882 to Margaret Ann Knott, born June 6, 1859, died January 6, 1916 in Washington, daughter of Stanislaus Knott (1793) and Elizabeth Harding. Her obituary states that they had four children. He was head of household in the 1900 census of the Eleventh District, for the town of Barnesville, with his wife Anna, married for nineteen years. She had been the mother of five children, four surviving and at home:
   (1) Roger Edward Jamison, born November 2, 1884.
   (2) Mary Lillian Jamison, born January 24, 1889
   (3) Leo Knott Jamison, born September 9, 1892
   (4) Dorothy Elizabeth Jamison, born April 28, 1895

c. Sophia Elizabeth Jamison, born c.1852, died c.1981; buried with her parents.

d. Teresa Ann Virginia Jamison, born June 15, 1855, died 1932; buried with her parents.

e. Francis Clinton Jamison, born July 28, 1858

f. Charles C. Jamison, born c.1860, died 1947; buried at St. Mary's Cemetery in Barnesville, with his wife. Married April 29, 1909 to Sarah Margaret Harris of Barnesville, born 1871, died 1948, daughter of Abraham Harris. They had at least:
   (1) An unnamed infant death, 1911.
   (2) Charles Harris Jamison, born May 28, 1911 at Dickerson in Montgomery County, died August 8, 1995 at Shady Grove Hospital near Rockville; buried at St. Mary's Catholic Cemetery, in Barnesville. Married November 7, 1942 to Laura Josephine Conlon of the District of Columbia, who was a commercial education graduate of Mary Washington College at Fredericksburg. Within three weeks of marriage, Charlie entered the Army, and served in the Philippines. Soon after coming home, Charlie bought part of *Stony Castle Estate* on Edward's Ferry Road, and over the years added several other farms to his holdings. Raised in the shadow of

Sugarloaf, Charlie often characterized himself as a "poor old mountain boy," but he was far more than that. A farmer, realtor, president of the county council, investor, developer, civic leader, and many other interests, he was all of that, but primarily a scrupulously honest man, with a friendly smile for everyone, who never forgot his heritage. Their children were:

(a) Charles Thomas Jamison, born January 20, 1946 while his father was in the Pacific.
(b) William H. Jamison.
(c) Robert P. Jamison.
(d) Frank Jamison.
(e) Laura M. Jamison, married to Griffin.
(f) Aimee E. Jamison.

(3) Margaret Jamison, married to Whitmore and lived at Lucketts, Virginia.

g. Eugene A. Jamison, born c.1871, died c.1943; buried at Bethesda United Methodist Church, Browningsville. Married December 19, 1899 to Exie King Purdum, daughter of Henning Purdum. At least one son:

(1) Charles H. Jamison, born 1904, died 1908, buried with his father.

2. Benjamin F. Harding, born c.1833. Head of household in the 1870 census of the Third District of Montgomery County, he was reported there as born c.1830, and a farmer, with $2,500 in real estate and $250 in personal property. He was married in the county by license dated January 26, 1864 to Mary Ann Howard, born c.1848. She appeared with him in the census, listed as Mollie A., and then with two children. Living in the household was Leonard Howard, born c.1799 and Drusilla Howard, born c.1813, who were apparently her parents. Also living in the household was Roberta Howard, born c.1852, and Leonard H. Howard, born c.1855, who were apparently Mary's brother and sister. The children were:

a. Laura M. Harding, born April 13, 1866 (records of St. Mary's Catholic Church, Rockville).
b. William C. Harding, born c.1867, of whom more.

3. Mary Virginia Harding, born April 18, 1836; baptized January 7, 1837. Records of St. John's Catholic Church at Forest Glen, Montgomery County.
4. Lloyd Joseph Harding, born c.1840, baptized November 1, 1854; records of St. Mary's Catholic Church, Rockville. Lloyd was head of household in the 1870 census of the Fifth District, with his sister Mary living with him. He was there reported as owning $5,000 in real estate and $100 in personal property. The surname was reported as Hardin. Head of household in the 1880 census of the Medley District of Montgomery County, Lloyd had his sister Mary still living with him, both being single. In the 1900 census of the Second District, we found the household of Lloyd Hardin (sic), there reported as a widower, born March, 1834, which is somewhat earlier than other records, if we are dealing with the same individual. Living with him was a daughter:
    a. Myrtle Hardin (sic), there reported as born October, 1885, and in school. Records of St. Mary's Catholic Church report the birth of Myrtle Harding on September 27, 1885, the daughter of Lloyd Harding and Laura Harding, of Barnesville.

## William C. Harding
## 1867-1957

This son of Benjamin F. Harding (1833) and Mary Ann Howard (1848), was born c.1867 in Montgomery County, died 1957; and was buried at Forest Oak Cemetery in Gaithersburg, with his wife. He is perhaps the same of that name and approximate birth year found as head of household in the 1900 census of the Eleventh District. He then had a wife Mary E., born May, 1877, married for seven years. She was Mary Ellen Howard, and had been the mother of four children, with two surviving, although three were listed. It appears that they had several children after the 1900 census, references being made to them in the obituary of one of those first three listed children. Mary Ellen died May 10, 1951 at Montgomery General Hospital, and had lived at 20 Summit Avenue, Gaithersburg; buried at Forest Oak Cemetery. The family apparently consisted of, at least:

1. William Thomas Harding, born April 9, 1894; records of St. Mary's Catholic Church at Barnesville and St. Rose's Church at Clopper. Lived at Buck Lodge when he was inducted July 23, 1918 at Rockville as private, 71st Infantry, Co G; discharged January 31, 1919. He was married to Exie May prior to army service, and had at least these children:
   a. William Thomas Harding, Jr., born May 29, 1921 at Boyds, died October 10, 1996 at his home; buried at Laytonsville Cemetery. The *Sentinel* reported that he was issued a marriage license about October 9, 1941 for marriage to Olive D. Phillips, born c.1923 of Washington. Other records indicate he married c.1944 to Hazel M. Smith, and was survived by his wife, a daughter, a nephew Kenneth Oglesbee of Frederick, three grandchildren, three great grandchildren, a sister and four brothers. He was a self-employed carpenter, and enjoyed hunting. Daughter and a son:
      (1) Kathy Harding, married Duvall; lived in Derwood. Her brother's obituary in 1985 lists her husband as Jefferson, of Derwood.
      (2) William Thomas Harding, III, born c.1945, and died November 11, 1985 in a hospital at Gainesville, Florida; buried at Laytonsville Cemetery. Like his father, he was a carpenter; survived by a son:
         (a) Thomas M. Harding of Frederick.
   b. Evelyn Harding, married to Hughes; lived in Virginia.
   c. Ernest Melvin Harding, born December 4, 1923 at Boyds and lived in West Virginia. T/3, USA, second world war; enlisted from Rockville.
   d. David Harding; lived in West Virginia.
   e. Benjamin Harding; lived in Florida.
   f. Joseph Harding; lived in Florida.
2. Annie Rebecca Harding, born September, 1896, died February 11, 1953 at Gaithersburg, Maryland; buried at St. Mary's Catholic Cemetery, Rockville. Married May 21, 1916 at Barnesville to Elmer Joseph Kuster of Dickerson, Maryland, son of Frederick W. Kuster. After the death of Elmer, she was married second April 4, 1947 to John Edward Fox, who died February 11, 1953 at Gaithersburg; buried at Forest Oak

Cemetery. His obituary lists two children, perhaps from a first marriage: Betty Fox and Dorsey Fox. She had children, including:

a. Elmer Joseph Kuster, Jr., died February 11, 1953 at his home on Russell Avenue in Gaithersburg; buried at the Clarksburg Methodist Cemetery. Survived by his widow, Elinor Louise, and children:
   (1) Ronald Joseph Kuster.
   (2) Rita Elaine Kuster.
   (3) Sharon Darline Kuster.
b. Alice Rebecca Kuster, married to Harmon.
c. Elinor Columbia Kuster, married to Beane.
d. Mamie Lucile Kuster, married to Lutz.
e. Robert Harrington Kuster.
f. William Clinton Kuster.
g. Joan Cecelia Kuster, married to Nelson.
h. Mary Ellen Kuster, married to Ralph Fitzwater.

3. John Edward Harding, born June 20, 1899, died March 5, 1963 at Montgomery General Hospital; buried at Forest Oak Cemetery in Gaithersburg. His obituary provides the names of several siblings, including his brother William T., the eldest, and all those younger than John Edward. He was married in the county to Violet J. Souders, born c.1914, died September 20, 2000 at Shady Grove Hospital near Gaithersburg from complications resulting from Parkinson's; buried at Forest Oak Cemetery. She was born at Darnestown, a daughter of Robert Souders and Maude Schwartzbeck. Violet was a fifty-year member of St. Martin's Catholic Church in Gaithersburg, and for many years was the baker for the cafeteria at Gaithersburg High School. John Edward and Violet had children, listed in the following order in the obituary of their mother, with places of residence as of 2000. There were also seventeen grandchildren and twenty great grandchildren, not listed:

a. Jean Harding, married to Charles Graham of Rockville.
b. Priscilla Ann Harding, married to Ronald Hansen of Gaithersburg.
c. Janet M. Harding, married John Burdette of Monrovia.
d. Jacqueline S. Harding.

e. Julia V. Harding, married to Gabor of Frederick.
f. Kenneth L. Harding, of Rockville; married Carole.
g. Carvel E. Harding, of Jefferson, in Frederick County, Maryland; married Janet.
h. Upton L. Harding, of Gaithersburg; married Constance.
i. Lita Joan Harding, predeceased her mother
j. John Edward Harding, Jr., predeceased his mother.
k. Robert L. Harding, predeceased his mother.

4. A. Vernon Harding, a son.
5. Mary Ellen Harding, born 1909, died 1989; married to Norman C. Groshon, born 1911, died 1984. Buried at Forest Oak Cemetery in Gaithersburg.
6. Debra R. Harding, born July 17, 1902; married to Albert Vernon Harding, born May 27, 1895, died July 29, 1964 at his home at 104 Waters Street, Gaithersburg; buried at Forest Oak Cemetery. His parents are not yet determined, but his obituary identifies several of his siblings: Elmer Harding; James Harding; Mrs. Minnie Heffiner; Mrs. Virginia Hoffler; Mrs. Aleuca Harding of Frederick; Mrs. Ivy Ashburg; and Harry Harding of Baltimore. Albert Vernon Harding lived at Adamstown, Frederick County, when he was inducted September 26, 1917 as a private, in Co L, 313$^{th}$ Infantry Battery D, 32$^{nd}$ Field Artillery. Advanced to corporal September 24, 1918; discharged December 9, 1918. Her obituary identifies her parents, her sister Alice Pumphrey, and her husband, and states that she died March 21, 1972 at Rockville, and was buried at Forest Oak Cemetery in Gaithersburg, leaving children, with place of residence as of the death of their mother. It also states that there were twenty-two grandchildren, thirty-four great grandchildren, and many nieces and nephews. The children were:
   a. Albert Vernon Harding, Jr., of Riviera Beach, Florida.
   b. Melvin Woodrow Harding of Wheaton. Born June 9, 1924 at Boyds, died June 6, 1995 at Rockville; buried at Forest Oak Cemetery in Gaithersburg. The obituary mentions several of his siblings, but no wife or other survivors.

c. Hazel Rae Harding, born c.1925; married in the county by license dated March 4, 1943 to Max Kelley Emerson of Rockville, born c.1924.
d. Ruth D. Harding, married to Kidwell of Ijamsville.
e. Doris A. Harding, married to Smith of Hyattstown.
f. Hannah M. Harding, of Germantown.
g. Charles B. Harding, of Washington.
h. Elizabeth L. Harding, married to Webb of Independence, Virginia.
i. Delores Y. Harding, married to Bell of Mount Airy.
j. James R. Harding, predeceased his mother.

7. Alice B. Harding, married Pumphrey; lived in Germantown. Perhaps married also to Dodd.
8. Benjamin Joseph Harding, born January 18, 1906, died March 13, 1979 at Suburban Hospital in Bethesda, Montgomery County; buried at Forest Oak Cemetery in Gaithersburg. He was Chief Quarterman of the grounds and roads of the National Naval Medical Center. Married at St. Martin's Catholic Church in Gaithersburg on July 18, 1966 to Ethel Shiflett, and was the father of several children, fifteen grandchildren and three great grandchildren. His children included:

a. Joyce Harding, married to Burdette; lived in Bakerton, West Virginia.
b. Gloria Harding, married Carter; lived at Rocky Ridge.
c. Shirley Harding, married to Burdette.
d. Pearl Harding, married to Payne.
e. Christine Harding, married to Bradshaw.
f. Benjamin Joseph Harding, Jr., born 1935, died 1937; buried at Forest Oak cemetery in Gaithersburg.

9. Upton David Harding, born c.1913, died February 11, 1953 at Gaithersburg; buried at Forest Oak Cemetery. Survived by his wife Ophelia Neal Harding, born 1929, died 1997; buried with her husband. He was a Pfc, USA, second world war, and had children:

a. Nancy Marie Harding.
b. Sharon Regenia Harding.

## Richard A. Harding
## 1803-

Head of household in the 1850 census of the Third District of Montgomery County, Richard was living about eleven dwellings removed from that of Lloyd F. Harding (1794), and purely by geographical and time frame, could have been another brother, but that is now only supposition.

Born c.1803 in Maryland, he was also a farmer, with $9,300 in real estate. Married in the county by license dated October 16, 1828 to Jemima W. Gittings, born c.1808 in Maryland. They then had seven children living at home. Living with them was Patrick H. C. Gittings, born c.1828, who owned $500 in real estate; and Henrietta M. Harwood, born c.1822. Head of household in the 1860 census of the Third District, Richard was listed with $6,750 in real estate and $1,300 in personal property. His wife Jemima was at home, with five children. Living with them was Henrietta Howard (sic), born c.1820, not otherwise identified.

We next found what we read as Richard J. Harding as head of household in the 1870 census of the Third District of Montgomery County, with the proper birth year, and his wife Jemima. He was then listed under the Barnesville Post Office, and was there reported as owning $7,500 in real estate and $1,623 in personal property, quite well-to-do for the time period. Listed in the household were two black servants, and four children were still at home. The children were:

1. John T. Harding, born c.1832; at home in 1860
2. Ann V. Harding, born c.1837; at home in 1860 and 1870
3. Richard N. Harding, born c.1840
4. Abraham J. Harding, born c.1842; at home in 1860 and 1870
5. Demaris G. Harding, a son, born c.1844; at home in 1860 and in 1870
6. Ernest H. Harding, born c.1848
7. Alda T. Harding, born c.1849
8. Gertrude P. Harding, born c.1853; at home in 1860 and 1870

# CHAPTER 8

## Robert Henry Harding
## 1825-

We first found this individual as head of household in the 1850 census of the Fourth District, although there he was listed as Robert H. Hardin (sic), born c.1825 in Virginia. He is the same individual, however, discussed here. His wife was then reported as Mary E., born c.1834, also in Virginia, and they then had the first three of their children.

Head of household in the 1870 census of the Fourth District of Montgomery County, he was listed as Henry Harding, born c.1822 in Virginia, and was a farmer with $300 in real estate. Having been born in Virginia, he is probably not of the direct lineage discussed earlier in our study, but his descendants appear in later county records, and are included here for that reason. His wife Mary E. was born c.1837, also in Virginia, and there were then seven children living at home.

Listed as Henry Harden (sic), he was head of household in the 1880 census of the Fourth District, with his wife Mary and eight children living at home. Some of the names appear to be second given names, and ages appear to be a bit different, but we are still dealing with the same family. As an example, Henry is now reported at the age of sixty-three years, or born c.1817, much earlier than reported in older census records. Mary is reported as born c.1838, very close to earlier reports.

Mary E. Harding, a widow, was found as head of household in the 1900 census of the Potomac District, born February, 1837 in Virginia. Two daughters were still living at home: Martha B. Harding, born June, 1870, and Carrie L. Harding, born August, 1880; both in Maryland.

Mary E. Harding died April 30, 1916 at the home of her son Louis in Georgetown, providing the name of one more child. Her *Sentinel* obituary states that she was survived by two sons and seven daughters, one of whom was Mrs. Magruder Ricketts of Rockville, thus clearly identifying the family. Children were born in Maryland, including:

1. William H. Harding, born October 25, 1855, died September 4, 1892; buried at Hermon Presbyterian Cemetery, with a son and a daughter. Probably the individual of that name married in the county July 26, 1883 to Roberta Jane Ricketts, born c.1858, daughter of Richard Edward Ricketts (1829) and Christian Anne Trail (1826). The *Sentinel* reported "William Harding died September 4, 1892 at Tennallytown (sic), D. C. from a gunshot wound, leaving his widow, a daughter of Richard E. Ricketts near Rockville, and five children." Not found in the 1900 census. Known children included:
   a. Virgie Harding, married first to Powell, and second to Harris.
   b. Amy Harding, married to West.
   c. Regina Connelly Harding.
   d. William Leroy Harding, born April 19, 1885, died May 14, 1885.
   e. Roberta C. Harding, born May 15, 1889, died May 22, 1889 at Marshall Hall, Charles County, Maryland (*Sentinel* notice).
2. Margaret J. Harding, born c.1857. Middle name apparently Jane from the 1880 census.
3. Sarah Catherine Harding, born January 24, 1860, of whom more following. Not at home in 1880
4. Frances Harding, born c.1860; not at home in 1880
5. Annie Harding, born c.1863, baptized August 24, 1867 at the age of four years (records of Rockville Methodist Church). Married in the county by license dated July 21, 1886 to William E. Gingell, but not found in the 1900 census of the county. Still at home in the 1880 census.
6. Eliza Harding, born c.1865; not at home in 1880. Baptized August 24, 1867 at age of three, residence listed as near Concord, Montgomery County (records of Rockville Methodist Church).
7. Laura Virginia Harding, born c.1867; at home in 1880. Baptized August 24, 1867 at age of five months, residence listed as near Concord, Montgomery County (records of Rockville Methodist Church).
8. Martha B. Harding, born June, 1870.

9. Tillie May Harding, baptized May 10, 1874 (records of the Rockville Methodist Circuit), daughter of Henry and Mary Harden (sic).
10. Louis Willoughby Harding, born c.1874, died November 1, 1928 at his home in Washington. Native of Montgomery County; survived by his wife, two daughters and a number of brothers and sisters. (*Sentinel*). At home in 1880 census. Baptized October 25, 1876 (records of Rockville Methodist Church).
11. Charles Franklin Harding, born August 31, 1877; named in obituary of his sister Sarah Catherine Harding Ricketts. Lived in Washington.
12. Carrie Lee Harding, born c.1880, died August 12, 1909 at the home of her sister, Mrs. W. E. Gingell of Georgetown. She was a sister also of Mrs. U. M. Ricketts, and the wife of Walter Hamilton of Cabin John. Survived by her husband and one three year old daughter, name not stated in *Sentinel* obituary.

**Sarah Catherine Harding**
**1860-1942**

This daughter of Henry Harding (1822) was born January 24, 1860 in Montgomery County and died April 5, 1942 at her home, buried at Rockville Union Cemetery. Her obituary in the *Sentinel* mentions three sisters by their married names, whom we have yet to identify: Mrs. Robert Morgan and Mrs. Nellie Nicholson, both of Washington; and Mrs. John Wenzel of Herndon, Virginia. Sarah Catherine was married as his second wife at Rockville, Montgomery County, Maryland May 22, 1884 to Ulysses Magruder Ricketts, born April 27, 1856, died January 17, 1931; buried Rockville Cemetery with his second wife. He was a son of Richard Edward Ricketts (1829) and Christian Anne Trail (1826) and was first married August 9, 1880 at Rockville to Mary Ella Davis, born c.1858 in the District of Columbia, died December 10, 1882 in Rockville as the result of a train accident, daughter of William M. Davis (1823). He and Sarah appeared in the 1900 census, Rockville Town, household # 126, with six children:
1. Mary E. Ricketts, born September, 1885, died August 18, 1970 at her home in Rockville, buried at Arlington National

Cemetery; having survived her husband. She was married to Orion Randolph Benson, and in 1966, lived at 210 Forest Avenue, Rockville. She was survived by two of her sisters; Katherine E. Dronenburg and Frances E. Ricketts: two granddaughters; Barbara Burdette Klix and Cynthia Corderman; and three children, daughter Edna having predeceased her mother:

a. Edna Benson, born c.1911, and died July 16, 1951 at home in Rockville. She was resident manager of the Blandford Apartments, employed by the Town Council office for some time, and the former Miss Rockville in 1941. Married to James L. "Dick" Burdette, born 1907, died September 12, 1984 at Shady Grove Hospital. He was a son of James Franklin Burdette (1870) and Iona M. Snyder (1878). After the death of Edna, James L. was apparently married second to Martha R. He was a retired police officer in Montgomery County, Maryland, and he and Edna had a daughter:
   (1) Barbara Burdette, born c.1940. Married Klix, and had children at Burke, Virginia:
      (a) Kathleen Klix.
      (b) Steven Klix.
      (c) Sharyn Klix.
b. Ella Mae Benson, married first to Corderman, and second to Bowman. At least one daughter:
   (1) Cynthia Corderman, married to Wildberger.
c. Katherine Rebecca Benson, born July 27, 1906, died April 30, 1994 at Rockville, single; buried at Neelsville Presbyterian Church cemetery.
d. Ralph Magruder Benson, born May 1, 1908, died May 31, 1979 at Rockville; buried at Neelsville.

2. Bessie E. Ricketts, born June, 1887.
3. Effie E. Ricketts, born September, 1888; married to Bradley Bell.
4. Katherine E. Ricketts, born November, 1890, married to Clifton Dronenburg; lived at 211 N. Van Buren Street, Rockville, in 1966.

5. Frances E. Ricketts, a daughter, born May, 1894; in 1966 living at 100 East Argyle Street, Rockville, single. Died February 27, 1980.
6. Eugene Washington Ricketts, born February, 1898 in Rockville, died February 20, 1966 at Casualty Hospital in Washington, D. C. He had retired in 1963 as chief clerk in the baggage department of Union Station, having served under eight station managers. Married August 6, 1918 to Margaret E. Viett, who survived him, with two children. She was a daughter of Albert D. and Amy Viett, named in the obituary of her mother which appeared in the July 22, 1937 issue of the *Sentinel*. Eugene's obituary also names three sisters surviving; Katherine, Mamie and Frances. His children, both living in Oxon Hill in 1966, were:
    a. Dorothy E. Ricketts, married Donovan.
    b. Eugene E. Ricketts, Jr.

# CHAPTER 9

## Harding Families of Frederick County

Not unexpectedly, several members of the family were also found in Frederick County, and will be included here. Those that have been identified within the principal families under study have been placed with those family groups, and will not be repeated.

### Mary A. R. Harding
### 1813-

We have not yet identified her parents, but Mary was born about 1813 in Maryland, probably Frederick County, and married there by license dated May 27, 1844 to William H. Thomas. He was found as head of household in the 1850 census of Frederick County for the Buckeystown District, born c.1812, and a farmer. They then had three children:

1. Sarah E. R. Thomas, born c.1845
2. Charles F. Thomas, perhaps a twin, born c.1849
3. Franklin C. Thomas, perhaps a twin, born c.1849

### Sarah Harding
### 1782-1855

Sarah was born c.1782 in Maryland, and was head of household in the 1850 census of Frederick County for Buckeystown District, and appeared to be a widow, owning $600 in real estate, with one son at home. Marriage records of Frederick County indicate that a license was issued dated February 13, 1807 between Sarah Ridgely and Lewis Harding, probably this family. Sarah left a will in Frederick County dated December 22, 1852, probated May 3, 1855, recorded in liber GH-1 at folio 54. In her will, she mentioned her deceased brother William Ridgley of Allegany County, providing an insight as to her maiden name. She expects to receive certain property from his estate and the will provides for its disposal to her children. There was no husband named, and only three children:

1. Mary Ann Harding, married to William Thomas. She received the negro woman Harriet and her sons Elias and John and her daughter Kitty, as slaves for life.
2. Lewis Ridgely Harding, born c.1816, listed in the census as the owner of five slaves, ranging in age from four to forty years; four females and one male. Under his mother's will, he received the negro slaves Jacob and Henry (sons of Harriet) and Maria, Rebecca and Ann, daughters of Harriet, with all the household goods and furniture, all the stock, and the harvested and standing crops. The will clarifies that he had remained with his mother after reaching his majority, managing the farm without compensation. Lewis was a small farmer, with 50 acres of improved land and 30 acres unimproved, valued at $600 total. He then owned 3 horses, 3 milch cows, 3 other cattle, 11 sheep and 12 swine. During the previous twelve months, he had produced 80 bushels of wheat, 150 bushels of Indian corn, 40 pounds of wool, 10 bushels of Irish potatoes, and 100 pounds of butter. He may be the same individual listed in the Jacob Engelbrecht Ledgers as L. Ridgley Harding, who died March 3, 1875 in Urbana District of Frederick County at the age of 58 years, 7 months and 23 days; buried at Mt. Olivet Cemetery in Frederick with his wife. Lewis R. Harding was married August 26, 1858 to Ann R. Leather, a daughter of Major John Leather. Ann was born c.1815 and died October 8, 1892; buried with her husband.
3. Ruth Harding, predeceased her mother. Her daughter received a cash legacy under the will of Ruth's mother:
   a. Elizabeth Catherine Michely.

## John B. Harding
## 1862-1923

This individual was an Episcopal Minister of Baltimore, born March 17, 1862 and died April 22, 1923, apparently in Frederick County. Married to Anna Mary Trail, born July 12, 1859, died July 18, 1942; buried at Mt. Olivet Cemetery in Frederick. She was a daughter of Colonel Charles Edward Trail (1825) and Ariana McElfresh (1828), youngest daughter of Colonel John Hammond McElfresh (1796) and Theresa Mantz (1794). Arianna died in Marseilles, France, while visiting her son Charles Bayard Trail (1857), then serving as United States Consul to France.

## Eleanor I. J. Harding
## 1803-

Eleanor was born about 1803 in Maryland, probably Frederick County, and was married there by license dated January 19, 1829 to Philip Mussetter. He was born January 5, 1798 and died January 25, 1875; buried at Kemptown Methodist Church. He was head of household in the 1850 census of Frederick County for the New Market District, with his wife and six children. Living with them was Margaret Mussetter, born c.1804, perhaps his sister. The children were:

1. Charles F. Mussetter, born c.1834
2. Lewis Mussetter, born c.1836, perhaps a twin
3. John Mussetter, born c.1836, perhaps a twin
4. Sarah Mussetter, born c.1838
5. Jane Mussetter, born c.1840
6. Michael Mussetter, born c.1843

## Christian Harding
## Died 1848

This individual left a will in Frederick County, dated October 11, 1848, probated November 6, 1848, recorded in liber GME-3 at folio 346. It is a lengthy will, leaving several different tracts of land to his children, and describing each of them by metes and bounds. Mentioned in the will was one Lydia Mealy, wife of Milton Mealy, not otherwise identified, but perhaps a daughter. There is no wife mentioned in the will, but he had several children, as follows:

1. Philip Harding, born October 28, 1794 in Maryland, who received the part of the farm on which his father then lived, containing 170 and ¾ acres, being part of the tract called *Establishment*; as well as 14 and 2/5 acres of the tract called *Darby's Delight*. Philip served as a private in the War of 1812 under Captain Denton Darby during 1814, and died August 16, 1877; buried at New London Methodist Church.

*Names In Stone* reports that his wife is buried with him, and gives her name as Rachel, which could be his first marriage. He was head of household in the 1850 census of Frederick County for the New Market District, and was a farmer, owning $6,000 in real estate. He was married in Frederick County by license dated March 14, 1846 to Rebecca Buckey, which was apparently his second marriage, based on the ages of the children listed in the household during the 1850 census. At that time, his wife Rebecca was listed, born c.1808, and there were four children at home. In the 1850 census, Philip was listed as owning 100 acres of improved land and 70 acres unimproved. He then owned 6 horses, 6 milch cows, 4 other cattle, 6 sheep and 20 swine. In the past year, he produced 500 bushels of wheat, 200 bushels of Indian corn, 40 bushels of oats, 30 bushels of Irish potatoes, 300 pounds of butter, 10 tons of hay and 8 bushels of clover seed. The James Engelbrecht Ledgers report that Rebecca died November 14, 1866 at 60 years old. Philip left a will in the county, dated July 5, 1871, probated November 3, 1877, and recorded in liber JRR 1 at folio 227. He is identified by his reference in the will to 170 acres of land "which I inherited from my father." His will named only three daughters, the youngest, presumably those born to his second marriage. His known children were:

a. Basil Harding, born March 26, 1830, died November 27, 1866; buried at New London Methodist Church in Frederick County, listed as a farmer, owning $3,000 in real estate in 1850, while living at home. Perhaps the same who was married in Frederick June 7, 1853 to Margaret E. Lowe, born c.1831, a daughter of John Lowe (born c.1785 in Delaware).
b. Margaret Harding, born c.1832, died December 30, 1864; perhaps Margaret Ann Harding, who was married in Frederick February 24, 1852 to Samuel Glisan, born August 17, 1825, died October 2, 1895; buried at New London Methodist Church with two wives and a son. Samuel was apparently married second to Mahala Shoup, born October 18, 1841, died August 25, 1904; buried with her husband. The son was apparently born to the first marriage; there could have been other children:

(1) William Barden Glisan, born c.1863, died March 19, 1871 at the age of 8 years, 9 months and 5 days.

c. Lucinda Catherine Harding, born c.1847; married in Frederick May 23, 1867 to John A. Meredith. She received a substantial cash legacy.

d. Anne Virginia Harding, born c.1849; married in Frederick County May 21, 1872 to Aloysius B. McCaffrey, born c.1837, son of Michael McCaffrey, a merchant, born c.1791 in Ireland. She received the 170 acres, with the stipulation that she pay certain sums to each sister.

e. Fannie B. Harding, who received a tract of 282 acres as purchased by her father from Basil D. Dorsey and Joseph Runkles. She was named as an Executor, which she renounced on November 12, 1877, signing the document as Fannie B. Burke, with Henry M. Burke, apparently by then her husband.

2. John Harding, who received three parcels of land under the will of his father. He received the farm on which he then lived, being 100 acres, part of *Darby's Delight* and part of *Peace and Plenty*. Also, part of *Establishment*, and 34 acres of *Drummine*. John also received another small parcel of 2 ½ acres of *Peace and Plenty*, as well as the house and two lots in the town of New Market. This is probably the same John Harding found as head of household in the 1850 census of Frederick County for the New Market District, this John Harding was born December 7, 1792 and was a farmer, with $5,000 in real estate. He was living next door to William Harding (1803), and was apparently a brother. He is probably the same John Harding who was married in the county by license dated March 25, 1820 to Hannah Norris, born March 26, 1793. Hannah was listed in the census as born c.1800, and they then had only one of their sons living with them, listed in a double household with his wife and a child. John served in the War of 1812 as a private under Captain Henry Riggs. John died February 7, 1872 and Hannah died February 20, 1875, and both are buried at Central Chapel Methodist Church, New London. John left a simple will in Frederick County dated August 8, 1863, probated March 19, 1872, recorded in liber SGC-1 at folio 246. He left his dwelling plan-

tation to his wife Hannah, and upon her death, to his son Oliver P. Harding. Their known son and a daughter were:

a. Oliver P. Harding, born August 27, 1822, died May 22, 1900; buried at New London Methodist Cemetery in Frederick County. Listed as head of household in the 1850 census of Frederick County for the New Market District, a farmer owning $3,000 in real estate, in a double household with his parents. Married in the county by license dated May 11, 1846 to Belinda E. Myers, born January 31, 1829, died September 22, 1918; buried with her husband. They had one child as of the 1850 census. Birth records of his children report the presence of Oliver P. Harding perhaps in Montgomery County, with a wife Belinda E. M. Harding (records of the Frederick Circuit, Methodist Church). She was born January 31, 1829, died September 22, 1918 and is buried with her husband. In the 1850 census, Oliver P. Harding was reported as owning 90 acres of improved land and 60 acres unimproved, valued at $6,000 in total. He owned five horses, 4 milch cows, 4 other cattle, 1 sheep and 27 swine. In the previous twelve months, he had produced 150 bushels of wheat, 50 bushels of rye, 250 bushels of Indian corn, 40 bushels of oats, 1,900 pounds of tobacco, 14 pounds of wool, 30 bushels of Irish potatoes, 300 pounds of butter, 10 tons of hay and 8 bushels of clover seed. The known children were:
    (1) Granville S. Harding, born August 12, 1847, died March 19, 1864 at Wyoming College, Kingston, Pennsylvania; buried with his parents.
    (2) Clayonia T. Harding, born July 7, 1852, died February 1, 1884; buried with her parents.
    (3) Everist C. Harding, born November 2, 1854
    (4) Hannah Mary Harding, born October 29, 1856, buried at New London Methodist Church.
    (5) John N. Harding, born September 2, 1859
    (6) Ardene Harding, reported as a daughter of O. P. Harding in the Jacob Engelbrecht Ledgers; married in Frederick County January 5, 1876 to William O. Hoffman.

b. Julia Ann Harding, born c.1824, died c.1837 at thirteen years.

3. William Harding, who received the grist mill and 51 acres on which he then lived, called *Dispute Continued.* He also was to receive the lot on which the old saw mill formerly stood which had recently been moved to the grist mill, containing just over an acre. This is probably the same William Harding who was found as head of household in the 1850 census of Frederick County for the New Market District, born c.1803 in Maryland, and was a miller, owning $4,000 in real estate. (Note that he inherited the mill near New Market from his father). In the census, he is reported as having a capital investment of $3,000, with raw materials valued at $500. His motive power is water, running two wheels, including a saw mill, with one male hand earning about eighteen dollars per month. He produced flour, rye chop and corn meal, with an annual production value of about $500. He is probably the same William Harding who was married in the county by license dated December 17, 1834 to Sarah Clary, born c.1812, and living with him at the time of the census, with seven children at home:

   a. Barbara Ann Harding, born c.1836; married in Frederick County March 25, 1860 to William Runkels.
   b. Sarah E. Harding, born c.1837
   c. Mary Jane Harding, born c.1839
   d. Cordelia E. Harding, born c.1841
   e. Columbus Harding, born c.1844
   f. Julia A. Harding, born c.1845
   g. Clara Harding, born c.1848

4. Christian Harding, Jr., deceased prior to his father. His children were named in the will to receive the farm called part of *Peace and Plenty*, containing 26 acres, and 2 ½ acres of the tract called *Norris' Purchase*. The children were:

   a. Basil Harding, died November 27, 1866 at Linganore.
   b. Margaret Ann Harding.

5. Solomon Harding, apparently another deceased son. There were some rather complicated provisions in the will relative to the payment of certain sums to or for the benefit of children of Solomon, deceased, named as being:

a. Elizabeth Ann Harding.
b. Mary Harding.
c. Thomas Harding.
d. Philip Harding.

In the course of research, we found several short items relative to Harding family members, that we have not yet associated with the families in the main body of the text. They are presented here for further analysis. All names in the left column bear the Harding surname, either by birth or marriage. All events occurred in Frederick County, unless otherwise specified.

| Individual | Event |
|---|---|
| Carlene P. | Born c.1827; with Ellen C. Harding, born c.1828. In the 1850 census of Fredericktown, both living in household of Eliza C. Gardner (1811). |
| Charlie | Born March 29, 1854, died October 27, 1866; buried at New London Methodist Church. |
| Ernest C. | Born 1854, died 1939; buried at Mt. Olivet in Frederick with wife Clara E. (Rice) Harding, born November 25, 1852, died March 18, 1931 |
| Fanny V. | Married in Frederick County November 10, 1887 to J. Marshall Miller. |
| Grace G. | Born August 14, 1855, died August 8, 1863; buried at Frederick Catholic Church. |
| Lewis D. | Married September 1, 1870 to Ella A. Barrick. |
| Sarah Ann | Married December 18, 1834 to George Hasselbach, son of John Hasselbach. |

# CHAPTER 10

## Miscellaneous Harding Families

In the course of research, references have been found to other members of the Harding family, which can not be matched with any of the groups discussed in earlier chapters. The information is presented here for further study.

### Mary E. Harding
### 1837-

In the 1880 census of Montgomery County for the Fifth District, we found a household headed by Josiah Bell, born c.1817 in Maryland. His wife was Mary E., born c.1817, and there were three children in the household. Josiah Bell was married in the county by license dated October 16, 1879 to Mary Ellen Harding, apparently her second marriage. The children were:

1. N. M. Harding, born c.1871, listed as a stepdaughter.
2. Alverda Harding, born c.1876, listed as a stepdaughter.
3. Rose L. Bell, born c.1879

### James E. Harding

Birth records of Potomac Methodist Church report the names of children of James E. Harding and his wife Bernice P. Harding. He is perhaps James Edward Harding, who served as SoM 3/c, USN, second world war, from Rockville. The children were:

1. Gail Yvonne Harding, born November 24, 1949 in Bethesda.
2. James E. Harding, Jr., born September 4, 1952 in Bethesda.

### George Warren Harding
### 1904-1990

The obituary of his wife provides most of what we now know about this individual, other than from personal knowledge. Present day family members have told me that George was born in Maine, and that his father was a ship captain. He is apparently not related at all to the Harding families generally discussed in the earlier chapters, but his family provides an excellent example of the need to look into each family found. As will be noted following, his daughter Kay (1834) married Washington Waters White, III. In that same family, Charles Thomas White (1933), brother of Wash, was married to Barbara Jeanette Harding (1933). At a brief glance, one might suspect that the two girls were sisters; in fact, there is no known relationship at all!

George Harding was born c.1904, and was engaged for many years in the cultivation of azaleas at his home on Wildcat Road near Gaithersburg. During the early years of development of the new town of Montgomery Village, he served as a consultant to the nursery division of Kettler Brothers, Inc., developers of the project, advising on all matters relative to plant material, selection, planting and conservation. I was Vice President of Land Development for the company at that time, and came to know and admire George quite well professionally. His wife was Cathryn Marguerite Sagrario, born April 22, 1908 in Washington, the daughter of Saturnino A. Sagrario and Susan Wynkoop. Catherine died February 23, 1995 at the Wilson Health Care Center in Gaithersburg, leaving twelve grandchildren, ten great grandchildren, and her children:

1. Betty S. Harding of Gaithersburg.
2. Kay H. Harding, February 6, 1934 at Washington, D. C. and married March 27, 1954 at Gaithersburg, to Washington Waters White, III, born March 1, 1929, baptized August 30, 1931 at St. Bartholomew's Episcopal Church in Laytonsville. He was a son of Washington Waters White, Jr. (1903) and Louisa Hood Griffith (1903). They had children, the first born in Montgomery County; the second in Washington, D. C.; and the last four in Leesburg, Virginia:
   a. Washington Waters White, born November 8, 1954. Married February 5, 1977 to Michele Cuseo, daughter of Michael Angelo Cuseo, Jr. and Donna Irene Thompson.
   b. George Warren White, born May 25, 1956. Married May 23, 1981 Susan Lynne Janney.
   c. John Michael White, born September 12, 1957. Married September 12, 1981 to Kimberly Dee Burdette, born

September 21, 1961, daughter of Allen Eugene Burdette (1938) and Shelva Jean Wright (1940).

d. William Wynkoop White, born February 14, 1959
e. Tracy Marguerite White, born April 13, 1961. Married Michael Watson.
f. Nancy Elizabeth White, born May 29, 1963.

3. Lynn Harding, married to Alger, of Bentonville, Virginia.
4. Warren S. Harding, of Bethesda.

## Samuel R. Harding
## 1839-1910

Family group sheets found in the library of the Montgomery County Historical Society in Rockville provide information about this individual. He was born c.1839 and died November 29, 1910; buried at Ivy Hill Cemetery, in Laurel, Prince George's County. He was married to Annie Catherine Tighe, born August 14, 1859, died October 12, 1938; buried with her husband. He was found as head of household in the 1900 census of the Laurel District of Prince George's County, with his wife and three daughters. Living with them were Robert Harding (1891), a nephew; and Peter Tighe (1860), a brother-in-law. Children:

1. Jessie May Harding, born September 25, 1881, died February 20, 1916. Married c.1906 at her parent's home to Samuel Townsend Moore, born February 19, 1891 at Norwood, son of Joseph Pigman Moore (1839) and Lacey Townsend. Joseph P. Moore was head of household in the 1900 census of the Fifth District, with his wife and five children, including Samuel, then nineteen years of age. However, Joseph's wife is there reported as Letitia J. Moore, born c.1858. *Marriage Licenses Montgomery County, Maryland 1798-1898*, by Janet Thompson Manuel, report the marriage of Joseph P. Moore by license dated February 27, 1877 to Lacey Townsend, and she appeared with her husband as Lacey in the 1880 census of the Fifth District. Samuel died August 25, 1962 at Olney, and was buried at St. Mark's Cemetery at Fairland. They had children:
   a. Evelyn Moore, born October 31, 1908, married Kevin T. Ryan.

b. Joseph Moore, born September 30, 1914, died c.1862. Married to Alma and had children:
   (1) Robert Moore.
   (2) Donald Moore.
2. Anna T. Harding, born c.1883 according to the census; buried at Ivy Hill, with no dates.
3. Frances Elizabeth Harding, born c.1892, died September 11, 1969. Married to Nelson Fisher, born 1886, died 1970.
4. Agnes Loretta Harding, born January 28, 1895 at Laurel, died March 28, 1972. Married January 6, 1922 to Harry Milton Carroll, born January 30, 1897 at Norwood, son of Clarence Benjamin Franklin Carroll (1869) and his wife, Carrie Virginia Turner (1873). No children.

**Theodore A. Harding**
**Died 1907**

Theodore left a will in Montgomery County dated October 31, 1907 at Washington, D. C., filed without probate in liber HCA 14 at folio 45, and later probated November 22, 1927, and recorded in liber PEW 9 at folio 254. The two filings appear to be the identical document and state that he died November 7, 1907. He names his wife Carrie as beneficiary and mentions his interest in the estate of his father in Binghamton, New York. Two sons are mentioned as beneficiaries upon the death of his wife:
1. Harry T. Harding.
2. Clarence L. Harding.

**Alice Elizabeth Harding**
**1923-**

Alice Elizabeth Harding was born August 14, 1923, and married August 25, 1945 at Kilmarnock, Virginia to Arthur Fletchall Woodward, born June 17, 1920 at Poolesville, a doctor. He was a son of Charles William Woodward (1895), Judge of the Circuit Court for Montgomery County, and Mary Clarinda Fletchall (1891). With her place of birth, Alice Virginia is probably not related to the families generally under study here. Children:
a. Nancy Harding Woodward: March 20, 1948.

b. Kathy Lemoine Woodward: May 19, 1949.
c. Diane Fletchall Woodward, born September 11, 1950
d. Arthur Fletchall Woodward, Jr., born December 14, 1951.

## William H. Harding
## 1816-

This William Harding was found as head of household in the 1860 census of the Fifth District of Montgomery County, born c.1816 in Maryland. He was a farmer, owning $1,000 in personal property, and he and other members of his family were of an age to have been found in the 1850 census of the county, had they been living there at that time. We read the name of his wife from the enumeration sheets as being Lohadian, born c.1823 in Maryland. However, we note that William Harding was married in the county by license dated May 29, 1840 to Lorada Ann Brown, which may have been the proper couple. She was born May 30, 1818 and died June 20, 1882. In any case, in the 1860 census, William appeared to be the father of eight children. Living in the household was William Johnson, born c.1814, a laborer. The children were:

1. Catherine Harding, born c.1842
2. Mary Elizabeth Harding, born September 23, 1842, died March 14, 1918 near Ednor, Montgomery County. Married December 20, 1866 to Andrew Jackson Thompson, born c.1839, died 1918, about fifty-one days prior to his wife. In the 1870 census of the Fifth District, we found a household headed by Benjamin Thompson, a farmer, apparently single, born c.1836. Listed with him was Andrew J. Thompson, his wife Mary E., and two children. Also living in the household was Minerva Harding, born c.1858, sister of Mary Elizabeth, and John Leizear, born c.1867, not yet identified. The two Thompson boys were brothers, having been found in the 1850 census of the First District of the county, living with their mother Ann Thompson (1816), who was apparently a widow. Listed by his initials as A. J. Thompson, he was head of household in the 1880 census of the Fifth District, with his wife Mary E. and seven children at home. Andrew was next found as head of household in the 1900 census of the Fifth

District, with his wife Mary E. and three children still at home. They had been married for thirty-three years, and she had been the mother of eleven children, all of them surviving. The obituary of Mary Elizabeth states that she was survived by four sons and seven daughters. She was also survived by forty-five grandchildren, ten great grandchildren, three sisters and three brothers. The children, with place of residence at the time of their mother's death, included:

a. Benjamin Howard Thompson, born c.1867;
b. Anne E. Thompson, born c.1869; married to Wilson and lived at Ridgewood, New Jersey.
c. Edith V. Thompson, born c.1871. In the 1900 census of the Ninth District, this daughter was listed as head of household, born June, 1871, single, and the mother of two children, both living with her. In her household was her sister Martha, there reported as born August, 1874, and also single. In her mother's obituary, she was reported as married to Poole, and lived at Burtonsville. The two children were:
   (1) John Thompson, born June, 1898
   (2) Infant boy Thompson, born May, 1899
d. Martha E. Thompson, born c.1873. Married in the county by license dated January 30, 1893 to Thomas L. Milstead and lived at Childs, Maryland. He was head of household in the 1900 census of the Fourteenth District, born July, 1871, with his wife Martha, although there her middle initial was read as L rather than E, reported born February, 1873. Married for seven years, she had been the mother of three children, all at home:
   (1) Vetrice I. Milstead, a daughter, born March, 1894
   (2) Dora E. Milstead, born April, 1895
   (3) Lester L. Milstead, born August, 1899
e. Mary Irene Thompson, born c.1875; married to Johnson and lived in Washington.
f. Granville J. Thompson, born c.1877, lived at Colesville. Head of household in the 1900 census of the Fifth District, he was living alone with his wife, Edna, born March, 1878, married for just two years.

g. Sarah J. Thompson, born c.1879. Married to Richardson and lived at Ednor, Maryland.
h. Herbert E. Thompson, born July, 1880; of Spencerville.
i. Lucy M. Thompson, married to Milstead of Spencerville; mentioned only in her mother's obituary.
j. Jessie L. Thompson, a daughter, born September, 1884; married to Kress and lived in Brooklyn, New York.
k. Almus C. Thompson, born May, 1887; a minister living in Youngstown, Ohio.

3. Martha Matilda Harding, born October 8, 1844; died December 26, 1916. Married December 26, 1877 to Anthony Boyd Poole, born May, 1854. He was head of household in the 1900 census of the Fifth District, a farmer, with Martha M. listed as born October, 1846. Married for twenty-two years, she had been the mother of three children, all at home:
   a. Thomas B. Poole, born December, 1878
   b. Luther C. Poole, born November, 1880
   c. Hannah E. Poole, born December, 1883
4. Minerva J. Harding, born c.1848. A child of this name and birth year was found in the 1870 census of the Fifth District, living in the household of Benjamin Thompson (1836). Married in the county by license dated May 18, 1873 to John Samuel Case, born April 12, 1850, died January 10, 1917 near Wheaton. He was a son of George L. Case (1822) and Elizabeth Beckwith (1827), both of whom were born in Germany, according to census records. John was head of household in the 1880 census of the Fifth District, with his wife Minerva, and one son. They were not found in the 1900 census of Montgomery County. The *Sentinel* obituary of John Samuel Case states that he was survived by his wife and three children. The one known child from the census was:
   a. Oliver Nimrod Case, born May 30, 1874, died October 16, 1903 in the Wheaton area. He had one child, and was buried at the Free Methodist Church at Layhill.
5. Josephine Harding, born c.1850; reportedly married October 15, 1871 to Henry Oden, although they were not found in marriage or census records of Montgomery County.
6. William H. Harding, Jr., born c.1853, died August 2, 1923. Married November 26, 1878 to Louisa Caroline Iager, born

c.1858, died c.1940 and had children. She was a daughter of Henry Aaron Iager and Mary E. Bergmann of Burtonsville. Children were:

a. Mary Ada Harding, born c.1879; married October 26, 1898 to John Robert Coar, born September, 1874 in Maryland. He was head of household in the 1900 census of the Fifth District, a merchant, with his wife Mary A., married for two years, and parents of one child. Living with them was Isaiah Coar, born November, 1816 in Pennsylvania, of an Irish father, listed as father; and Charles H. Harding, reported there as born February, 1871, but perhaps her brother. The child was:
   (1) Ellen C. Coar, born September, 1899
b. Mary Laurette Harding, born November 3, 1880.
c. Charles Henry Harding, born February 8, 1882, and died c.1947
d. Melvin Randolph Harding, born August 30, 1884, died July 10, 1889; records of St. Paul Lutheran Church at Fulton, Howard County.
e. Jeanette Crighton Harding, born December 19, 1886. Married May 28, 1912 to Albert W. Brady.
f. Ethel Elizabeth Harding, born April 8, 1892. Married February 22, 1915 to William C. Judy. A daughter:
   (1) Virginia Judy, married to Adolphus Gordon.

7. Charles Nimrod Harding, born February 1, 1855, died May 3, 1925. Married November 26, 1879 at Ellicott City, Maryland to Margaret Botterel, and had children. He was head of household in the 1900 census of the Fifth District of Howard County, with his wife Margaret, born January, 1844, and two of their children. The children included:
   a. Ella May Harding, died April 17, 1932. Married January 31, 1900 to Charles Hewlett Wallick.
   b. Montella Roby Harding; married to Lillian Brown.
   c. Arthur M. Harding, born c.1886, died c.1934
   d. Virginia Olivia Harding, born July 15, 1880.
8. Samuel Thomas Harding, born April 13, 1858, died November 14, 1924; buried at Union Cemetery, Burtonsville, with his wife. Married February 8, 1881 to Martha Elizabeth Poole of Spencerville, born November 14, 1859, died January,

1946; daughter of Mahlon Poole and Susan Brown. He left a will in the county dated November 22, 1916, probated December 2, 1924, recorded in liber PEW 9 at folio 276, naming his wife Martha. She left a will dated August 23, 1944, probated February 13, 1946, recorded in liber OWR 14 at folio 260, in which she named her daughters Lottie and Hattie, and a granddaughter. She had at least three children, her son predeceasing his mother:

a. Hattie Lee Harding, born c.1882, buried at Burtonsville; married January 3, 1906 at Liberty Grove Methodist Church, Burtonsville, to Henry J. Krouse and had at least one child, named in the will of her grandmother:
   (1) Mary E. Krause.
b. Lottie Mae Harding, born August 30, 1887 at Spencerville; married April 26, 1900 at Liberty Grove Methodist Church, Burtonsville, to Clarence Herbert Wright.
c. Richard Thomas Harding, born August 23, 1891 in Washington, died October 24, 1916 at Burtonsville. Buried with his parents.

## Edward J. Harding
## 1889-1940

Records of St. John's Catholic Church at Forest Glen indicate that this individual is buried there, born c.1889, and died 1940. His wife Marie Ruth Harding is buried with her husband, born c.1893 and died c.1964. Also buried with them is his sister, E. Catherine Harding, born c.1898, died c.1973. Edward J. Harding left a will in Montgomery County, dated August 31, 1935, probated October 22, 1940, and recorded in liber HGC 33 at folio 279. The filing reports that he died on October 5, 1940. He left his entire estate to his wife, Marie Ruth Harding, and in the event of her prior or joint death, to their two children. He then provided that, should his wife and both his children predecease him, four-fifths of his estate was to go to his mother Julia Ann Harding of Plainfield, New Jersey, and one-fifth to his sister-in-law, Margaret Jaeger, also of Plainfield. In the event that his wife and children predecease him, he named his mother and a brother, Lewis R. Harding as Executors. The two children were:

1. Anais Ruth Harding.
2. Edward J. Harding, Jr.; perhaps the Edward Joseph Harding who was an Ensign in the United State Navy during the second world war, inducted from Silver Spring, Montgomery County.

In the course of research, we found several short items relative to Harding family members, that we have not yet associated with the families in the main body of the text. They are presented here for further analysis. All names in the left column bear the Harding surname, either by birth or marriage. All events occurred in Montgomery County, unless otherwise specified.

| Individual | Event |
|---|---|
| Ann | Born c.1776, died in March, 1850 of pleurisy, listed as a widow in the First District. |
| Byron Everson | Died August 6, 1957; buried Darnestown Presbyterian Church cemetery. Beverly Ann Harding died on the same day, also buried there. He was a Lt. (jg), USN, serving from Mt. Rainier in Montgomery County during the second world war. |
| Charles | Born c.1889, died June 11, 1924 at the home of his father, John Harding, near Darnestown. |
| Charles Leroy | Sergeant, US Marine Corps, second world war, from Rockville. |
| Christiana | Born c.1825 in Maryland; living in the household of Samuel S. Briggs (1813) during the 1850 census for the Rockville District. |
| Clara | Born c.1866; listed with Charles Harding, born c.1868. In the 1880 census of the Fifth District, both listed in the household of James L. Dorsey (1842), reported as niece and nephew. |
| Clarence | Born May, 1871 in New York, an artist. Head of household in the 1900 census of Bethesda District, with wife Rena P., born June, 1872 in Washington, and two children also born there: |

| | |
|---|---|
| | Lowell S. Harding, born August, 1894; and Dorothy H. Harding, born December, 1896. |
| Cora | Married April, 1877 at Relay House, B&O Railroad, to Buth Frizzell. Records of Frederick Circuit, Methodist Church. |
| Cosmos M. | Died January 29, 1919; buried at Monocacy Cemetery at Beallsville. |
| Darrell Lee | Seaman, first class, USN, second world war, from Silver Spring. |
| Eddie B. | Born February 15, 1899, died October 19, 1961 at Travilah. Wife C. Louise, born November 19, 1907. Darnestown Presbyterian. |
| Edgar W. | T/4, USA, second world war; of Green Acres, Montgomery County. |
| Edward T. | Born September, 1874 in Iowa, of parents born in England; listed as a traveling salesman, and a brother. In the 1900 census of the Bethesda District, living in the household of Louisa A. Earl, a widow, born September, 1857 in Ohio. |
| Edward Wood | Lt. Colonel, USA, second world war; Wood Acres, Montgomery County. |
| Elizabeth | Born c.1829 in Maryland; listed as a weaver and apparently with a son Joseph Harding, born c.1857. In the 1860 census of the Fifth District, both living in the household of Nancy Thompson (1785). Perhaps the same Elizabeth, of the proper birth year, found in the 1880 census of the Fourth District, listed as divorced, and living in the household of James Shaw (1808) and his wife Eliza Shaw (1810). |
| Elizabeth T. | Elizabeth Thompson Harding, died March 15, 1915; buried at Rockville, unmarked. |
| Ella S. | Married by license dated April 8, 1890 to William H. Mullican. Not found in 1900 census. |
| F. A. | Born c.1830, died July 8, 1921 at his daughter's home in Kensington. Ret. Colonel, USA. |
| Georgeanna | Born July, 1834; married in the county by license dated January 11, 1870 to Edward Penn, born November, 1839. He was head of house- |

| | |
|---|---|
| | hold in the 1900 census of the Fourteenth District, with his wife. Married for thirty years, they had been childless. |
| Harold Friend | Colonel, USA, second world war; of Takoma Park. |
| Harry Augustus | Baptized October, 1903; records of Clarksburg Methodist Church. |
| Henry | Died June, 1863; buried at Rockville. |
| Hugh L. | Pfc, USA, second world war; of Chevy Chase. |
| Jane | Born c.1825, received first communion April 27, 1837 at the age of twelve; at St. John's Catholic Church at Forest Glen. |
| John C., Jr. | 1st Lieutenant, USA, second world war; from Bethesda, Montgomery County. |
| John Edgar | Sgt, USA, second world war; of Silver Spring. |
| John H. | Married December 16, 1828 to Rachel Bond at St. Peter's Episcopal Church, Poolesville. |
| John S. | Born c.1853 in Maryland; in the 1880 census of the Seventh District, living in the household of Lester D. Moore (1845). |
| John Thornley | Lieutenant, USN, second world war; Bethesda. |
| Keturah | Married September 30, 1824 William H. Hays. St. Peter's Episcopal Church, Poolesville. |
| Lee | Married October 22, 1938 in the Presbyterian parsonage at Germantown to Virginia Dorsey, daughter of G. Slagle Dorsey. |
| Lee Nathaniel | Seaman 1/c, USN, second world war; from Rockville. |
| M. E. | Born August 12, 1844, died April 8, 1882; buried in Harding family cemetery at Cloverly. Sex not reported. |
| Mable G. | Born June, 1867 in Ohio, a widow; head of household in the 1900 census of the Bethesda District, with Dorothy Harding, born May, 1888 in the District of Columbia; and Kammerer Harding, born February, 1896 in the District; and Mary Kammerer, born February, 1837 in Ohio, her mother. |

| | |
|---|---|
| Margie M. | Died June 5, 1898 at seven days of age. Daughter of William and Mary E. Harding; St. Mary's, Barnesville. |
| Mary Jane | Born c.1927, died January 25, 1971 at Holy Cross Hospital, daughter of William Harding. Buried at Mt. Carmel Cemetery, Sunshine. |
| Maybel | Born 1901, died August 8, 1901 at aged found months and thirteen days. Union Cemetery at Burtonsville. |
| Michael Eugene | Born December 17, 1935, died March 15, 1936 and buried at Forest Oak in Gaithersburg. |
| Norman L. | Pfc, USA, second world war; of Laurel. |
| Norman Leo | Born March 11, 1891, died December 11, 1892 son of N. B. and L. Harding. Buried Mt. Olivet in Frederick. |
| Peyton | Born c.1792 in Virginia; listed as a laborer in the household of Jonathan W. Fields (1820) during the 1850 census of Rockville District. |
| Richard | Married January 8, 1824 to Elizabeth Ann Brown; both of Montgomery County. Records of St. Bartholomew's Episcopal Church. |
| Robert Lee | Born September 11, 1914 at Germantown, died December 8, 1989 at the Frederick Memorial Hospital. His obituary mentions only his wife, Virginia D. Harding. |
| Robert Mervin | AS, USN, second world war; of Chevy Chase. |
| Samuel Herbert | Of Highland in Howard County, born c.1873, died 1919, buried at St. John's in Forest Glen. Married October 15, 1901 to Marian L. Boyle in Washington at the home of her father, Lt. Richard B. Boyle (1848). He died at his home in Washington May 17, 1919 leaving his wife and several children. (*Sentinel* obituary). |
| Samuel S. | Born 1911, died 1936; Neelsville Presbyterian Church cemetery. |
| Solomon E. | Lived in Washington; died September 1, 1966; reportedly buried at Mt. Olivet Cemetery. H was a brother of Mary Chappel; Beatrice War- |

| | |
|---|---|
| | gowski; Mabel E. Osthaus; George H. Harding and Francis Harding. |
| Thomas I. | Died April 15, 1975 at Washington Adventist Hospital. Husband of Josephine I. Harding, and father of Thomas I. Harding, Jr. |
| Wallace Edward | Married December 14, 1909 in the rectory of Christ Episcopal Church, Rockville, to Rock Homa (?). |
| William | Born February, 1867 in Maryland, single. In the 1900 census of the Eighth District, listed as brother-in-law, living in the household of William L. Purvis (1860) and his wife Emily (1863). |
| William C. | Of Kensington; married July 22, 1916 Deborah E. Bowman of Wheaton, daughter of William J. Bowman. William C. was born May 29, 1893, died March 31, 1978 at Germantown. Deborah was born August 27, 1896, died May 21, 1963 at Sibley Hospital. |
| William E. | Pvt, USA, second world war; of Germantown. |
| William Edward | Of Germantown; married at Grace Episcopal Church, Woodside on October 8, 1937 to Mary Marjorie Keating, the daughter of M. Frank Keating of Forest Glen. |
| William Ellsworth | Born April 27, 1890 in Montgomery County; inducted July 23, 1918 as private, 154 Dep. Brigade, Co. G, 17th Infantry, USA. Honorably discharged January 31, 1919. |

# BIBLIOGRAPHY


Allnutt, Anne C. *Allnutt, Chiswell, Darby, Dawson, White.* Genealogy Database Printouts. 1996. Library of the Montgomery County Historical Society. Rockville, Maryland.

Andrews, Mathew Page. *Tercentenary History of Maryland.* Three volumes. Chicago & Baltimore. S. J. Clarke Publishing Co. 1925.

Aud, Kathleen L. and Susan E. *Our Ancestors,* 1972, Washington, D. C. Federal Lithography Co. Privately published. Montgomery County Historical Society library, Rockville, Md.

Baltz, Shirley V. & George E. *Prince George's County, Maryland, Marriages and Deaths in Nineteenth Century Newspapers. Volumes 1 and 2.* Bowie, Md. 1995. Heritage Books, Inc.

Barnes, Robert. *Maryland Marriages, 1634-1777.* Baltimore, Md. Genealogical Publishing Co. Fifth printing 1995.

_____. *Maryland Marriages, 1778-1800*

_____. *Marriages and Deaths From the Maryland Gazette 1727-1839.* Baltimore. Genealogical Publishing Co. 1973

_____. *Colonial Families of Anne Arundel County, Maryland.* Westminster, Maryland: Family Lines Publications, 1996.

_____. *Marriages and Deaths from Baltimore Newspapers.* Three volumes. Baltimore. Genealogical Publishing Co. 1978

Barnes, Robert W. and F. Edward Wright. *Colonial Families of the Eastern Shore of Maryland, Volumes 1 and 2.* Westminster, Md. Family Line Publications. 1996

Barrow, Healan and Stevens, Kristine. *Olney: Echoes of the Past.* Westminster, Maryland. Family Line Publications. 1993.

Boggs, Ardith Gunderman. *Goshen, Maryland, A History & Its People.* Bowie, Md. Heritage Books, Inc. 1994

Bowie, Effie Gwynn. *Across The Years in Prince George's County.* Baltimore, Md. Genealogical Publishing Company. Original 1947. Reprint 1996.

Boyd, T. H. S. *The History of Montgomery County, Maryland.* Clarksburg, Md 1879. Reprint Baltimore, Md. Genealogical Publishing Co., Inc. 1989, 1996, 1998

Broderbund Software, Inc. *Family Tree Maker, Deluxe Edition III.* Social Security Death Index, Volumes 1 and 2; and World Family Tree, Volumes 1 thru 52. Redwood, California. 1997

Brown, Helen W. *Index of Marriage Licenses, Prince George's County, Maryland 1777-1886.* Baltimore, Md. Genealogical Publishing Co. Reprint. 1995

______. *Prince George's County Maryland Indexes of Church Registers 1686-1885, Volume 2.* Westminster, Md. Family Line Publications. 1994

Brumbaugh. *Maryland Records.* 1915 and 1928 issues; Washington County Marriages.

_______. *Maryland Records, Colonial, Revolutionary, County and Church.*

Burke, Sir Bernard, Ulster King of Arms. *The General Armory of England, Scotland, Ireland and Wales, Volumes 1, 2 & 3..* Bowie, Md. Heritage Books, Inc. 1878, Reprint 1996

Buxton, Allie May. *Nehemiah Moxley, His Claggettsville Sons and Their Descendants.* Chelsea, Michigan. BookCrafters. 1989

Carothers, Bettie Sterling. *1776 Census of Maryland.* Westminster, Md. Family Line Publications. 1992

Carroll County Genealogy Society, Md. *Carroll County Cemeteries, Volume Three: Southwest.* Westminster, Maryland 1992.

Cavey, Kathleen Tull-Burton. *Tombstones and Beyond, Prospect U. M. Church Cemetery and Marvin Chapel Church Cemetery.* Westminster, Maryland: Family Lines Publications, 1995

Chapman. *Portrait and Biographical Record of the Sixth Congressional District, Maryland.* Chapman Publishing Company, New York. 1898

Church of Jesus Christ of Latter Day Saints. *Family group sheets, computerized ancestral files, International Genealogical Index, and other pertinent records.* Family History Center, Silver Spring, Maryland.

Coldham, Peter Wilson. *The Bristol Register of Servants Sent to Foreign Plantations 1654-1686*, Genealogical Publishing Company, Baltimore. 1988

________. *The Complete Book of Emigrants, 1607-1660,* Genealogical Publishing Co., Baltimore, 1987

________. *The King's Passengers to Maryland and Virginia.* Westminster, Maryland. Family Line Publications 1997.

Cook, Eleanor M. V. *Guide to the Records of Montgomery County, Maryland, Genealogical and Historical.* Westminster, Md. Family Line Publications. 1997

___________, *Notes Concerning Facts, Allegations and Gossip in Divorce Cases 1820-1894, Montgomery County, Maryland*. Privately printed. Montgomery County Historical Society Library. 1995.

___________, *Apprenticeship Records, Montgomery County, Maryland, 1779-1840*. Privately printed. Montgomery County Historical Society Library. 1994.

Cuttler, Dona and Michael Dwyer. *The History of Hyattstown.* Bowie, Md. Heritage Books, Inc. 1998

___________, *The History of Comus,* Bowie, Md. Heritage Books, Inc. 1999.

___________, *The History of Barnesville and Sellman,* Bowie, Md. Heritage Books, Inc. 1999.

___________, *The History of Dickerson, Mouth of Monocacy, Oakland Mills, and Sugarloaf Mountain*. Bowie, Md. Heritage Books, Inc. 1999.

___________, *The Cemeteries of Hyattstown*. Bowie, Md. Heritage Books, Inc. 1999.

___________, *Montgomery Circuit Records, 1788-1988.* Bowie, Md. Heritage Books, Inc. 1999.

___________, *The Genealogical Companion to Rural Montgomery Cemeteries.* Bowie, Md. Heritage Books, Inc. 2000

Darby, Rodney H. *All About Darbys*, Privately published, Rockville, Maryland. 2000

Day, Jackson H. *James Day of Browningsville, and his descendants, A Maryland Family.* Columbia, Md, private printing, 1976.

Dern, John P. and Mary Fitzhugh Hitselberger. *Bridge in Time, The Complete 1850 Census of Frederick County, Maryland.* Redwood City, CA. Monocacy Book Company. 1978

Eader, Edith Oliver & Trudie Davis-Long. *The Jacob Engelbrecht Marriage Ledger of Frederick County, Maryland 1820-1890.* Monrovia, Md. Paw Prints, Inc. 1994.

________. *The Jacob Engelbrecht Death Ledger of Frederick County, Maryland 1820-1890.* Monrovia, Md. Paw Prints, Inc. 1995.

________. *The Jacob Engelbrecht Property and Almshouse Ledgers of Frederick County, Maryland.* Monrovia, Md. Paw Prints, Inc. 1996.

Ferrill, Matthew & Gilchrist, Robert. *Maryland Probate Records 1635-1777.* Volume 9.

Fleming, Bertha Ann. *The Brandenburg Family in America.* Not published; private compilation deposited with the Frederick County, Maryland, Historical Society.

Flowers, Susanne Files & Edith Olivia Eader. *The Frederick County, Maryland Will Index 1744-1946.* Monrovia, Md. Paw Prints, Inc. 1997

Frain, Elizabeth R. *Monocacy Cemetery, Beallsville, Montgomery County, Maryland.* Lovettsville, Va. 1997, Willow Bend Books.

Fry, Joshua & Jefferson, Peter. *Map of Virginia, North Carolina, Pennsylvania, Maryland, New Jersey 1751.* Montgomery County, Md Library, Atlas Archives.

Gaithersburg, Maryland, City. *Gaithersburg, The Heart of Montgomery County.* Privately printed. 1978

Gilland, Steve. *Frederick County Backgrounds.* Westminster, Maryland: Family Lines Publications, 1995.

_______. *Early Families of Frederick County, Maryland and Adams County, Pennsylvania.* Westminster, Maryland: Family Lines Publications, 1997.

Green, Karen Mauer. *The Maryland Gazette, Genealogical and Historical Abstracts, 1727-1761.* Galveston, TX The Frontier Press. 1989

Gurney, John Thomas, III. *Cemetery Inscriptions of Anne Arundel County, Maryland. Volume 1* . Pasadena, Md. Anne Arundel Genealogical Society. 1982, 1994.

_________. *Cemetery Inscriptions of Anne Arundel County, Maryland. Volume 2.* Chelsea, MI. BookCrafters. 1987

Haney, Ritchie Lee. *1920 Census for Damascus, Montgomery County, Maryland.* From personal notes of his father, Ritchie E. Haney, census-taker. Damascus, Md. Private. 1997

Hartzler, Daniel D. *Marylanders in the Confederacy.* Westminster, Maryland: Family Lines Publications, 1994.

Holdcraft, Jacob Mehrling. *Names in Stone; 75,000 Cemetery Inscriptions From Frederick County, Maryland.* Ann Arbor,

Michigan. 1966. Reprinted with "More Names in Stone" in two volumes, Genealogical Publishing Co., Baltimore, 1985

Hopkins, G. M. *Atlas of Fifteen Miles Around Washington, Including the County of Montgomery, Maryland.* Baltimore, Md. Garamond/Pridemark Press, Inc. for the Montgomery County Historical Society. Original 1879. Reprint, 1975

Hurley, William N., Jr. *1850 Census of Montgomery County, Maryland.* Bowie, Md. Heritage Books, Inc. 1998

_____. *1860 Census of Montgomery County, Maryland.* Bowie, Md. Heritage Books, Inc. 1998

_____. *1870 Census of Montgomery County, Maryland.* Bowie, Md. Heritage Books, Inc. 1998

_____. *1880 Census of Montgomery County, Maryland.* Bowie, Md. Heritage Books, Inc. 1999

_____. *1900 Census of Montgomery County, Maryland.* Bowie, Md. Heritage Books, Inc. 2000

_____. *Our Maryland Heritage Series.* (See page iv for listings). Bowie, Md. Heritage Books, Inc. 1997-2000

Jourdan, Elise Greenup. *The Land Records of Prince George's County, Maryland, 1710-1717*

______. *Early Families of Southern Maryland. Volumes 1 through 6.* Westminster, Md. Family Line Publications. 1993 to 1998

Lord, Elizabeth M. *Burtonsville, Maryland Heritage, Genealogically Speaking.* Montgomery Co. Historical Society Library

Malloy, Mary Gordon; Sween, Jane C.; Manuel, Janet D. *Abstract of Wills, Montgomery County, Maryland 1776-1825* Westminster, Md. Family Line Publications. 1989, 1998

Malloy, Mary Gordon; Jacobs, Marian W. *Genealogical Abstracts, Montgomery County Sentinel, 1855-1899.* Rockville, Md. Montgomery County Historical Society. 1986.

Manuel, Janet Thompson. *Montgomery County, Maryland Marriage Licenses, 1798-1898.* Westminster, Md. Family Line Publications. 1987, 1998

Maryland State. *Archives of Maryland*, all volumes.

Maryland Hall of Records. *Wills, estates, inventories, births, deaths, marriages, deeds and other reference works relative to counties of Maryland.*

______. *Maryland Calendar of Wills.* All volumes.

______. *Maryland Historical Society Magazine.*

______. *Vestry Book of St. John's Episcopal Parish Church, 1689-1810.* Original.

Maryland Historical Society, War Records Division. *Maryland in World War II, Register of Service Personnel.* Two volumes. Baltimore. 1965

Maryland War Records Commission. *Maryland in the World War 1917-1919, Military and Naval Service Records.* Two volumes. Baltimore. 1933.

Meyer, Mary Keysor. *Divorces and Names Changed in Maryland By Act of the Legislature 1634-1867.* Mt. Airy, Md. Pipe Creek Publications, Inc. 1991

Montgomery County Court Records. *Wills, inventories of estate, deeds.* Rockville, Maryland.

Montgomery County Historical Society, Rockville, Maryland. *Folder files; census, church, correspondence, newspaper, manuscripts, library, and family records.*

Myers, Margaret Elizabeth. *Marriage Licenses of Frederick County, Maryland 1778-1810.* Westminster, Md. Family Line Publications. Second Edition, 1994

______. *Marriage Licenses of Frederick County, Maryland 1811-1840.* Family Line Publications. 1987

______. *Marriage Licenses of Frederick County, Maryland 1841-1865.* Family Line Publications. 1988

Newman, Harry Wright. *Anne Arundel Gentry, A Genealogical History of Some Early Families of Anne Arundel County, Maryland. Volumes One, Two and Three.* Annapolis, Md. Privately printed. 1979

________. *Charles County Gentry.* Baltimore, Md. Genealogical Publishing Co. 1971 and 1990 reprints from 1940 original publication.

________. *Mareen Duvall of Middle Plantation.* Private printing 1952. Baltimore, Md. Port City Press, Inc. Reprint 1984

Omans, Donald James and Nancy West. *Montgomery County (Maryland) Marriages 1798-1875.* Compiled by Potomack River Chapter, National Society of Colonial Dames. Athens, Georgia. 1987. Iberian Publishing Co.

Peden, Henry C., Jr. *Revolutionary Patriots of Prince George's County 1775-1783.* Westminster, Md. Family Line Publications. 1997

________. *Revolutionary Patriots of Montgomery County 1776-1783.* Westminster, Md. Family Line Publications. 1996

________. *Quaker Records of Southern Maryland, Births, Deaths, Marriages and Abstracts from the Minutes, 1658-1800.* Westminster, Md. Family Line Publications. 1992

Powell, John W. *Anne Arundel County, Maryland Marriage Records 1777-1877.* Pasadena, Md. Anne Arundel Genealogical Society. 1991

Prather, E. Jack. *Thomas Prather 1604-1666, Descendants and Allied Kin.* Evansville, Indiana. Evansville Bindery, Inc. 1995

Prince George's County, Md Genealogical Society. *Index to the Probate Records of Prince George's County, Maryland, 1696-1900.* Bowie, Md. 1989.

______. *Prince George's County Land Records, Volume A, 1696-1702.* Bowie, Maryland, 1976

______. *1850 Census, Prince George's County, Maryland.* Bowie, Maryland, 1978

______. *1828 Tax List Prince George's County, Maryland.* Bowie, Maryland, 1985.

Reinton, Louise Joyner. *Prince George's County, Md. Piscataway or St. John's Parish (now called King George's Parish. Index to Register, 1689-1878.*

Ridgely. *Historic Graves of Maryland and the District of Columbia*

Russell, Donna Valley. *Western Maryland Genealogy.* Volumes 1 thru 12. Catoctin Press, Middletown, Md. 1985-1996

___________, *Selby Families of Colonial America.* Middletown, Maryland, Catoctin Press, 1990.

Sargent. *Stones and Bones, Cemetery Records of Prince George's County, Maryland.*

Scharff, J. Thomas. *History of Maryland.* Three Volumes. Hatboro, Pennsylvania. Tradition Press. 1967

________. *History of Western Maryland, Volume 1.* Baltimore, Md. Genealogical Publishing Co., Inc. 1995

________. *History of Western Maryland, Volume II.* Baltimore, Md. Genealogical Publishing Co., Inc. 1995

________. *History of Western Maryland, Index to Volumes I and II.* By Helen Long (which see). Baltimore, Md. Genealogical Publishing Co., Inc. 1995

Schildknecht, Calvin E. *Monocacy and Catoctin, Volumes 1 thru 111.* Gettysburg, Pa. 1994

Skinner, V. L., Jr. *Abstracts of the Prerogative Court of Maryland, 1726-1729*

Tracey, Grace L. and Dern, John P. *Pioneers of Old Monocacy, The Early Settlement of Frederick County, Maryland 1721 to 1743.* Baltimore. Genealogical Publishing Co. 1987

Warfield, J. D. *The Founders of Anne Arundel and Howard Counties, Maryland.* Baltimore. Kohn & Pollock. 1905. Reprinted 1995, Heritage Books, Bowie, Md.

Weiser, Frederick Sheely. *Records of Marriages and Burials in the Monocacy Church in Frederick County, Maryland, and in the Evangelical Lutheran Congregation in the City of Frederick, 1743-1811.* National Genealogical Society. 4th Printing, 1993

_______. *Frederick, Maryland Lutheran Marriages and Burials 1743-1811.* Washington, D. C. National Genealogical Society. Fourth printing, 1993

Welsh, Luther W., A.M., M.D. *Ancestral Colonial Families, Genealogy of TheWelsh and Hyatt Families of Maryland and Their Kin.* Lambert Moon Printing Co., Independence, Missouri. 1928.

Western Maryland Genealogy. *Frederick County (Md) Wills, Unprobated Wills, Will Book A1, 1744-1777.* Middletown, Md.

Williams, T. J. C. & Folger McKinsey. *History of Frederick County, Maryland, Volume 1.* Baltimore, Md. Genealogical Publishing Co., Inc. 1997

_______. *History of Frederick County, Maryland, Volume 2.* Baltimore, Md. Genealogical Publishing Co., Inc. 1997

Williams, Thomas J. C. *History of Washington County, Maryland, Volume 1.* Baltimore, Md. Genealogical Publishing Co., Inc. 1992

_______. *History of Washington County, Maryland, Volume 2.* Baltimore, Md. Genealogical Publishing Co., Inc. 1992

Wright, F. Edward. *History of Washington County, Maryland, Index to Volumes 1 and 2.* Westminster, Md. Family Line Publications. 1992, 1995

________. *Anne Arundel County Church Records of the 17th and 18th Centuries.* Westminster, Md. Family Line Publications. 1989, 1994

________. *Marriages and Deaths in the Newspapers of Frederick and Montgomery Counties, Maryland. 1820-1830.* Westminster, Maryland: Family Lines Publications, 1992.

________. *Marriages and Deaths From the Newspapers of Allegany and Washington Counties, Maryland.* Westminster, Md. Family Line Publications. 1993

________. *Newspaper Abstracts of Frederick County 1811-1815.* Westminster, Md. Family Line Publications. 1992

________. *Newspaper Abstracts of Frederick County, 1816 to 1819.* Westminster, Maryland: Family Line Publications, 1993

________. *Newspaper Abstracts of Allegany and Washington Counties 1811-1815.* Westminster, Md. Family Line Publications. 1993

________. *Maryland Eastern Shore Vital Records, Book 1, 1648-1725.* Westminster, Md. Family Line Publications. 1993

________. *Maryland Eastern Shore Vital Records, Book 2, 1726-1750.* Westminster, Md. Family Line Publications. 1993

________. *Maryland Eastern Shore Vital Records, Book 3, 1751-1775.* Westminster, Md. Family Line Publications. 1993

________. *Maryland Eastern Shore Vital Records, Book 4, 1776-1800.* Westminster, Md. Family Line Publications. 1994

________. *Maryland Eastern Shore Vital Records, Book 5, 1801-1825.* Westminster, Md. Family Line Publications. 1994

________. *Washington County, Maryland Church Records of the 18th Century, 1768-1800.* Westminster, Md. Family Line Publications. 1988

________. *Bible Records of Washington County, Maryland.* Westminster, Md. Family Line Publications. 1992

________. *Frederick County Militia in the War of 1812.* Westminster, Md. Family Line Publications.

________. *Maryland Militia War of 1812, Volume 7, Montgomery County.* Westminster, Md. Family Line Publications. 1986

# INDEX

All names appearing in the text have been indexed, with reference to each page on which they appear. Most names appear with a date, generally indicating date of birth, in order to differentiate between individuals having the same given name. In some cases where birth dates are not available, dates of marriage or death will appear, such as m/1825 or d/1876. In the case of common names such as John or Mary, where no date is specified, the references are without question to more than one individual.

Berry, Rhiannon Leigh, 97
Bissett, Beverly June 1925, 60
Bissett, Cora I. 1892, 60
Bissett, James Ernest 1905, 60
Bissett, John E. 1894, 60
Bissett, John William 1868, 60
Bissett, William D. 1897, 60
Blair, No given name, 102
Bogley, Erma Helen Maria 1888, 58
Bogley, William A., 58
Bond, Carrie, 20
Bond, Rachel, 144
Bonner, Mae Carlyle 1904, 50
Boring, Edna Mae 1897, 96
Boring, George Washington, 96
Bosely, Cynthia Ann 1956, 41
Bosely, Robert A., 41
Boswell, Alexander Franklin 1818, 55
Boswell, Mary Elizabeth 1848, 55, 63
Botterel, Margaret 1844, 140
Bowling, Frank Augustus, 88
Bowling, Thelma 1919, 88
Bowman, Bessie T. 1923, 103
Bowman, Carrie Belle 1888, 84
Bowman, Deborah E. 1896, 146
Bowman, John, 103
Bowman, No given name, 122
Bowman, Perry G. 1850, 84
Bowman, Thelma, 103
Bowman, William J., 146
Boxall, Thomas, Jr., 78
Boyle, Marian L., 73, 145
Boyle, Richard B. 1848, Lt., 145
Bradshaw, No given name, 117
Brady, Albert W., 140
Branch, No given name, 40
Branch, Perry W., 40
Bready, William, 85
Breeding, No given name, 88
*Briarley*, 46
Briggs, Marie Frances 1908, 104
Briggs, Samuel S. 1813, 142
Brigham, Annie Emily 1917, 81
Broaddus, Emma L., 39
Brooke, Dorothy, 5
Brown, Elizabeth Ann, 145
Brown, Fortunate M. 1806, 73
Brown, Ida J., 87
Brown, James Howe, Jr., 44
Brown, Lillian, 140
Brown, Lorada Ann 1818, 137
Brown, Martha Ann 1843, 73
Brown, Robert 1790, 73
Brown, Susan, 141
Browning, Martha Letitia 1859, 93
Browning, William, 93
Bryan, James Ellis, 85
Bryant, Sarah, 90
Bucey, John Arthur, 41
Bucey, Randolph D., 41
Buckey, Rebecca 1808, 128
Buckler, John Robert 1948, 97
Buellert, Mark, 32
Buellert, Mark, Jr. 1983, 32
Buice, Pegeen Willa, 81
Burdette, Allen Eugene 1938, 135
Burdette, Barbara 1940, 122
Burdette, James Franklin 1870, 122
Burdette, James L. 'Dick' 1907, 122
Burdette, Jean Evelyn 1927, 67
Burdette, John, 115
Burdette, John D. 1875, 99, 100
Burdette, Kimberly Dee 1961, 134
Burdette, Martha R., 122
Burdette, No given name, 117
Burgess, Cora, 74
Burgess, Edward, Captain, 7
Burke, Henry M., 129
Burton, Lucy Jeanetta, 86
Burton, Richard A. 1845, 83
Bussard, John R., 36

Cook, John, 22
Cooke, Rachel, 33
Cooley, Alice F., 109
Cooley, John F., 109
Corderman, Cynthia, 122
Corderman, No given name, 122
Costello, Sarah Bridget 1903, 65
Counselman, Amanda 1841, 36
Counselman, Benjamin Franklin 1847, 35
Counselman, Benjamin J. 1849, 36
Counselman, Charles 1807, 35
Counselman, Hannah E. 1847, 36
Counselman, Henrietta 1841, 36
Counselman, Hester A. 1844, 36
Counselman, John 1805, 35
Counselman, John 1853, 36
Counselman, John Mines 1849, 35
Counselman, Louisa Virginia 1845, 36
Counselman, Lucy A. M. 1837, 36
Counselman, Samuel 1769, 35
Counselman, Samuel 1850, 36
Counselman, William G. 1839, 36
Covati, Matthew Warren, 66
Covati, No given name, 66
Covati, Stephanie Amber, 66
*Cowpen*, 4
Cronin, Rose Cecelia, 31
Cross, James 1803, 76
Crowley, Ann, 21
Crowley, No given name, 102
Crowley, Vincent, 21
Culver, Elizabeth 1773, 23
Culver, George H. 1854, 91
Culver, Virginia 1883, 91
Cuseo, Angelo, Jr., 134
Cuseo, Michele, 134
Dailey, Hannah A. 1856, 50, 52
Danoff, Emma Seton 1975, 66
Danoff, Lucy Caroline 1979, 66
Danoff, William Thomas, 66
Darby, Denton, Captain, 127
*Darby's Delight*, 127, 129
Daugherty, Betty Virginia 1928, 86
Daugherty, Robert, 86
Davis, Chantal Nicole, 97
Davis, Donald, 96
Davis, Eleanor, 2
Davis, Gordon Lee, Jr., 97
Davis, Heather Anne, 97
Davis, Kimberly Beth, 97
Davis, Kirk Gordon, 97
Davis, Mary Ella 1858, 121
Davis, Misti Lee, 97
Davis, Ryan Patrick, 97
Davis, Sean Kennedy, 97
Davis, William, Sr. 1694, 2
Dawes, Benjamin B., 38, 53
Dawes, Muriel Elizabeth 1829, 38, 53
Dawes, Rebecca 1798, 53
Day, Louisa E. 1824, 79
Day, Willia Green 1897, 43
Dayhuff, Charles Hal, 47
Dayhuff, Charles Hal, III 1937, 47
Dayhuff, Charles Hal, Jr. 1907, 47
Dayhuff, Jane Duke 1940, 47
Dayhuff, Marian Alicia 1935, 47
Deakins, Francis, Colonel, 108
Dellman, Wilhemina, 48
Denall, Samuel, 51
Diebert, Edward Harding, 29
Diebert, Joseph W., 28
Dierkoph, William, 77
*Discovery*, 4
Disney, Charles Tippett, 95
*Dispute Continued*, 131
Dodd, No given name, 117
Dominowski, Celestine 1923, 66
Donovan, No given name, 123
Dorsey, Basil D., 129
Dorsey, G. Slagle, 144
Dorsey, James L. 1842, 142
Dorsey, Virginia, 144

Dorst, Louisa M. 1820, 39
Dove, William T. 1891, 14
Doyle, William P., 58
Drane, Thomas O., 9
Dronenburg, Clifton, 122
Dronenburg, Katherine E., 122
Dronenburg, Lorraine 1920, 44
*Drummine*, 129
Dudley, Thelma Rene 1921, 74
Duke, Monette, 47
Duley, No given name, 102
Dunscomb, Lucy Claiborn 1773, 24
Duval, Ophelia, 11
Duvall, No given name, 114
Duvall, Samuel, 51
Dwyer, Clara Eva 1860, 54
Dwyer, Henry Pierce 1820, 54
Earl, Louisa A. 1857, 143
Ecker, No given name, 103
Edmonston, Archibald, 5
Edmonston, Jane, 7
Edmonston, Margery, 2
Edmonston, Thomas, 5
Edwards, Fred, 45
Edwards, Leonard B. 1899, 72
Elko, Louisa 1939, 65
Emerson, Max Kelley 1924, 117
Entwhistle, Thomas W., 18
*Establishment*, 127, 129
*Estep*, 83
Evans, Nancy Ann 1763, 4
Eveley, Rebecca, 51
Fairall, No given name, 6
Fannon, Anna Marie 1912, 65
Fausnaught, May, 41
Ferris, Lucille, 44
Fields, Jonathan W. 1820, 145
Filbey, Charles Albert 1909, 50
Filbey, Donna Lynn 1961, 50
Fink, No given name, 29
Finnance, Ernest, 94
Finnance, Letitia Marie, 95
Finnance, Martin Barnard, 94
Fisher, Albert Ambrose 1884, 58
Fisher, Alcesta Ann 1847, 54
Fisher, Allison, 65
Fisher, Andrew Geary 1904, 65
Fisher, Anna Lucille 1902, 56
Fisher, Annie 1874, 59
Fisher, Annie Emma Agnes 1876, 59
Fisher, Artaxerxes 1860, 62
Fisher, Belva Romaine 1903, 56
Fisher, Cecelia Elizabeth 1878, 57
Fisher, Cecelia Elizabeth 1919, 58
Fisher, Charles F. d/1972, 55
Fisher, Cherry Lee 1955, 41
Fisher, Christine Lee 1951, 66
Fisher, Constantia 1854, 60
Fisher, Craig Scott 1950, 41
Fisher, Dethia 1847, 59
Fisher, Dorothy Lee 1912, 56
Fisher, Douglas Vincent 1947, 65
Fisher, Edmund Ernest 1842, 59
Fisher, Elizabeth Catherine, 67
Fisher, Elizabeth Delight 1885, 58
Fisher, Elizabeth S., 57
Fisher, Ella L. 1879, 61
Fisher, Ella William 1910, 56
Fisher, Emma Delight 1862, 63
Fisher, Emma Viola 1885, 61
Fisher, Ernest E. 1886, 63
Fisher, Eva Editha 1887, 60
Fisher, Eva Stella 1881, 57
Fisher, Evelyn Aloysius 1902, 64
Fisher, Everard Geary 1824, 38, 53
Fisher, Everard Geary, Jr. 1851, 60
Fisher, Geary Aloysius 1873, 56, 63
Fisher, Geary Lawrence 1940, 65
Fisher, Glenna Elizabeth 1896, 55
Fisher, Gussie D. 1885, 58
Fisher, Helen Agatha 1898, 64

Fisher, Helen Lane 1879, 61
Fisher, Helen Marie, 58
Fisher, Ida M. 1884, 63
Fisher, Ida Theresa 1880, 57
Fisher, Ira T. 1880, 57
Fisher, Isaac U. 1896, 63
Fisher, Isadora Teresa 1880, 57
Fisher, Isadora W. 1861, 54
Fisher, Jacob Spencer 1894, 59
Fisher, James 1881, 60
Fisher, James Spencer 1894, 59
Fisher, Jessie Theckla 1907, 65
Fisher, John Franklin Millard 1872, 55
Fisher, John Norman 1908, 65
Fisher, John Norman, Jr. 1941, 65
Fisher, John Warren, 65
Fisher, Joseph E. 1914, 57
Fisher, Joseph Eldridge 1883, 57
Fisher, Joseph Milton 1905, 65
Fisher, Keith Perry 1959, 41
Fisher, Lawrence Gregory 1936, 65
Fisher, Lawrence Prescott 1903, 65
Fisher, Laywood L. 1888, 63
Fisher, Lee R. 1890, 61
Fisher, Leland Lawrence 1891, 58
Fisher, Leslie Ann 1952, 66
Fisher, Linda Anne 1846, 65
Fisher, Lois Ann 1949, 66
Fisher, Louis M. 1886, 61
Fisher, Lydia Elizabeth 1822, 48
Fisher, Margaret E., 56
Fisher, Margaret Lee 1915, 56
Fisher, Marie J. 1895, 55
Fisher, Mariel 1888, 61
Fisher, Mariel Editha 1850, 59
Fisher, Mariel Genevieve 1874, 56
Fisher, Marion 1870, 63
Fisher, Martha 1852, 61
Fisher, Mary Caroline 1900, 64
Fisher, Mary Constance 1949, 65
Fisher, Mary Edna 1913, 66
Fisher, Mary Elsa, 65
Fisher, Mary Magnolia 1871, 60
Fisher, Mary Margaret 1887, 58
Fisher, Mary Rose 1882, 61
Fisher, Maud Elizabeth 1882, 63
Fisher, May 1870, 59
Fisher, Michael Alan 1954, 66
Fisher, Millard Clay 1848, 55, 63
Fisher, Millard M. 1898, 55
Fisher, Nancy Lee, 66
Fisher, Nelson 1886, 136
Fisher, Patricia Marie 1955, 66
Fisher, Patrick Geary, 65
Fisher, Percy 1890, 63
Fisher, Philip Adrian 1912, 65
Fisher, Richard L., 58
Fisher, Robert Edward 1940, 65
Fisher, Rossey 1894, 63
Fisher, Ruth Adelaide 1907, 56
Fisher, Sam C., 41
Fisher, Samuel Edmund 1872, 59
Fisher, Samuel M. 1815, 59, 60
Fisher, Stanley Albert 1944, 65
Fisher, Stanley Eustace 1889, 58
Fisher, Thomas 1782, 48, 53
Fisher, Thomas M., 58
Fisher, Thomas V. 1884, 60
Fisher, Thomas Warren 1921, 66
Fisher, William Michael, 65
Fisher, William Thomas 1876, 56
Fitzwater, Ralph, 115
Fleming, Sarah Ann, 28
Fletchall, Mary Clarinda 1891, 136
Flook, Amanda, 80
Florance, Hazel 1896, 55
Florance, Henry R. 1895, 55
Florance, Richard H., 55
Fontaine, Sallie 1882, 43
Ford, Cassandra, 107
Ford, John 1720, 107
*Forrest*, 7

Foster, Lois Jean 1926, 66
Foster, Roy M., Colonel, 66
*Fox Race Ground*, 108
Fox, Betty, 115
Fox, Dorsey, 115
Fox, John Edward, 114
Fraley, Lois 1930, 101
Frizzell, Buth, 143
Gabor, No given name, 116
Gall, Bonny, 96
Gall, John, 96
Gall, Margaret, 97
Gamble, Joan Griffith 1938, 44
Gamble, Townley 1908, 44
Ganas, Andrew Constantine, 90
Ganas, Miltides Aristotle, 89
Ganas, Vic, 90
Gardner, Eliza C. 1811, 132
Garner, Norman Oldham, 94
Gatton, Edward W., 107
George, Elizabeth Ann 1947, 65
George, Forest Milburn 1903, 65
George, Michael Clair 1943, 65
George, Sarah Gail 1945, 65
Gibson, Catherine A., 94
Gibson, Eleanor Mae, 94
Gill, Elizabeth Perry 1929, 42
Gill, Everett, III 1931, 42
Gill, Everett, Jr., 42
Gill, Jane Rachel 1933, 42
Gill, Stephen Truex, 42
Gingell, William E., 120
Gittings, Jemima W. 1808, 118
Gittings, Patrick H. C. 1828, 118
Gittings, Thomas 1786, 38
Glass, Johanna, 47
Glass, Robert R., Colonel, 47
Glisan, Samuel 1825, 128
Glisan, William Barden 1863, 129
Gonder, Thomas E., 30
Gordon, Adolphus, 140
Graham, Bridgett 1827, 108
Graham, Charles, 115
Graham, Rachel 1828, 69
Granger, Rachel Louise, 42
Gray, Richard 1876, 60
Gregory, No given name, 101
Griffin, Linda Marie 1940, 48
Griffin, No given name, 112
Griffin, Paul K., 48
Griffith, Charles Howard 1907, 43
Griffith, Charles Howard, Jr. 1931, 44
Griffith, Gladys, 66
Griffith, Howard 1954, 44
Griffith, Howard G. 1879, 43
Griffith, Isobel 1959, 45
Griffith, James LaMond 1946, 44
Griffith, Laura 1961, 45
Griffith, Louisa Hood 1903, 104, 134
Griffith, Lucinda 1938, 45
Griffith, Mabel Elizabeth 1912, 44
Griffith, Margaret Waters 1910, 44
Griffith, Mary Ann 1921, 45
Griffith, Mary Patricia 1948, 45
Griffith, Pamela 1947, 45
Griffith, Thomas Perry 1913, 44
Griffith, William Barnstable 1918, 45
Groshon, Norman C. 1911, 116
Gunton, Mary Moylan, 13
Guthrie, Ruth 1781, 6
Hall, John H., 28
Hall, Mary Gladys, 96
Hall, Sarah Ann Fleming, 28
Hall, Sheila Ann Marie 1943, 66
Hall, Sophia M. 1794, 110
Hamilton, America Elizabeth 1845, 40
Hamilton, Walter, 121
Hammrick, Kelly, 32
Haney, Isabel, 58
Hannum, Carol Ann 1938, 47

Hannum, Christopher Paul 1962, 48
Hannum, Mary Alice 1943, 48
Hannum, Paul Craig 1908, 47
Hannum, Paul Craig 1940, 48
Hannum, Thomas Perry 1950, 48
Hansen, Ronald, 115
Harding, A. Vernon, 116
Harding, Abraham J. 1842, 118
Harding, Ada N. 1880, 73
Harding, Addie V. 1879, 99, 100
Harding, Adrian Wesley 1928, 80
Harding, Agnes 1896, 31
Harding, Agnes Loretta 1895, 136
Harding, Albert Alexander 1872, 80
Harding, Albert Vernon 1895, 116
Harding, Albert Vernon, Jr., 116
Harding, Alda T. 1849, 118
Harding, Aleuca, 116
Harding, Alice B., 117
Harding, Alice Elizabeth 1923, 136
Harding, Alice Lorraine 1923, 85
Harding, Alice R. 1847, 30
Harding, Alton L. 1905, 87
Harding, Alverda 1876, 133
Harding, Amelia, 9
Harding, Amelia Ann, 9
Harding, Amy, 120
Harding, Anais Ruth, 142
Harding, Andrew J. 1849, 83
Harding, Andrew Jackson 1830, 73, 83
Harding, Ann 1776, 142
Harding, Ann V. 1837, 118
Harding, Anna, 3, 9
Harding, Anna Marie 1927, 104
Harding, Anna T. 1883, 136
Harding, Anne Virginia 1849, 129
Harding, Annie 1863, 120
Harding, Annie Gertrude, 91
Harding, Annie Rebecca 1896, 114
Harding, Annie V. 1875, 100
Harding, Ardene, 130
Harding, Arthur Eugene 1871, 87
Harding, Arthur M. 1886, 140
Harding, Asbury 1814, 69, 99
Harding, Barbara A. 1836, 131
Harding, Barbara Jeanette 1933, 104, 134
Harding, Barrett Lee 1948, 88
Harding, Basil, 9, 131
Harding, Basil 1829, 128
Harding, Belinda E. M. 1829, 130
Harding, Benjamin, 114
Harding, Benjamin 1765, 3
Harding, Benjamin F. 1833, 112, 113
Harding, Benjamin Joseph 1906, 117
Harding, Benjamin Joseph, Jr. 1935, 117
Harding, Bentley Leroy 1910, 84
Harding, Bentley Milton 1880, 74
Harding, Bernice, 32
Harding, Bernice P., 133
Harding, Bertha 1879, 77
Harding, Bertha Irene 1896, 86
Harding, Bessie 1879, 77
Harding, Betty S., 134
Harding, Beverly Ann, 142
Harding, Birdy, 31
Harding, Blanche Emma 1874, 80
Harding, Brawner Zachariah, 103
Harding, Buddy E., 103
Harding, Byron Everson, 142
Harding, C. Louise 1907, 143
Harding, Carlene P. 1827, 132
Harding, Carol Ann 1956, 89
Harding, Carol Jane 1958, 87
Harding, Carole, 116
Harding, Caroline Frances 1793, 7, 14, 15

Harding, Edward T. 1874, 143
Harding, Edward Wood, 143
Harding, Edward, Jr., 7, 16
Harding, Elaine, 32
Harding, Eleanor, 30
Harding, Eleanor F., 107
Harding, Eleanor I. J. 1803, 127
Harding, Eleanora, 30
Harding, Elias, 3
Harding, Elias 1728, 6, 33
Harding, Elias d/1832, 107, 108, 110
Harding, Elias d/1838, 9, 24
Harding, Eliza 1865, 120
Harding, Elizabeth, 1, 6, 9, 31, 107, 108, 111
Harding, Elizabeth 1713, 3
Harding, Elizabeth 1758, 9, 33, 39
Harding, Elizabeth 1799, 8
Harding, Elizabeth 1824, 73, 93
Harding, Elizabeth 1829, 143
Harding, Elizabeth 1901, 31
Harding, Elizabeth A. 1853, 78
Harding, Elizabeth Ann, 132
Harding, Elizabeth Ann 1815, 14
Harding, Elizabeth B. 1895, 86
Harding, Elizabeth Ellen 1842, 25
Harding, Elizabeth L., 117
Harding, Elizabeth L. 1809, 27
Harding, Elizabeth Thompson d/1915, 143
Harding, Ella Lee 1871, 77
Harding, Ella May, 140
Harding, Ella May 1890, 82
Harding, Ella S. m/1890, 143
Harding, Ellen, 3, 24
Harding, Ellen C. 1828, 132
Harding, Elmer, 116
Harding, Elmer Lee 1892, 102
Harding, Eloise T., 105
Harding, Elsie May 1900, 29
Harding, Elsie Virginia 1888, 85
Harding, Elwood Lee 1918, 88
Harding, Emaline, 107
Harding, Erman Granville 1896, 86
Harding, Ernest C. 1854, 132
Harding, Ernest Elmo 1880, 80
Harding, Ernest H. 1848, 118
Harding, Ernest Melvin 1923, 114
Harding, Ethel Elizabeth 1892, 140
Harding, Ethel Mae 1894, 87
Harding, Eva Cornelia 1902, 87
Harding, Evelyn, 114
Harding, Everist C. 1854, 130
Harding, Exie May, 114
Harding, F. A. 1830, Colonel, 143
Harding, Fannie B., 129
Harding, Fanny V. m/1887, 132
Harding, Frances, 103
Harding, Frances 1860, 120
Harding, Frances Elizabeth 1892, 136
Harding, Francis, 146
Harding, Francis B. 1910, 105
Harding, Francis B., Jr., 105
Harding, Francis V. 1849, 24
Harding, Frank 1861, 30
Harding, Frank Myers 1900, 86
Harding, Gail Yvonne 1949, 133
Harding, Gary, 1, 5
Harding, George 1724, 6
Harding, George Davis 1869, 28
Harding, George H., 146
Harding, George Phillip 1842, 25
Harding, George Warren 1904, 133
Harding, George Washington 1810, 25
Harding, Georgeanna 1834, 143
Harding, Gertrude L. 1891, 31
Harding, Gertrude P. 1853, 118
Harding, Gladys Irene 1916, 84
Harding, Gloria, 117
Harding, Gloria 1937, 104

Harding, Gloria Lee, 85
Harding, Goldie Stenna 1886, 77
Harding, Grace G. 1855, 132
Harding, Granville 1851, 78, 79
Harding, Granville Jackson 1867, 84
Harding, Granville S. 1847, 130
Harding, Grove 1729, 11
Harding, Guy Marshall 1888, 29
Harding, Hannah M., 117
Harding, Hannah Mary 1856, 130
Harding, Harold, 30
Harding, Harold Alvin 1930, 89
Harding, Harold Ernest 1924, 80
Harding, Harold Friend, 144
Harding, Harold Harry 1908, 89
Harding, Harry, 116
Harding, Harry Augustus 1903, 144
Harding, Harry Geisbert 1874, 88
Harding, Harry T., 136
Harding, Harvey, 91
Harding, Harvey Leon 1881, 77
Harding, Hattie Lee 1882, 141
Harding, Hazel Rae 1925, 117
Harding, Hazel Virginia 1909, 74
Harding, Helen, 31
Harding, Helen J., 105
Harding, Helen M., 105
Harding, Henrietta 1873, 30
Harding, Henrietta Maria, 24
Harding, Henrietta W. 1868, 24
Harding, Henry 1782, 7, 12, 13, 16, 22
Harding, Henry 1822, 121
Harding, Henry d/1863, 144
Harding, Henry G. 1874, 88
Harding, Herbert Lee 1889, 85
Harding, Horace Albert 1898, 86
Harding, Hugh L., 144
Harding, Ida L. 1865, 100
Harding, Idabel 1873, 77
Harding, Jacqueline Leigh 1954, 89
Harding, Jacqueline S., 115
Harding, James, 116
Harding, James E., Jr. 1952, 133
Harding, James Edmond 1893, 31
Harding, James Edmond, Jr., 31
Harding, James Edward, 133
Harding, James Edward 1867, 28, 30
Harding, James Edward 1943, 32
Harding, James Edward, Jr. 1970, 32
Harding, James Henry 1868, 86
Harding, James Lee 1963, 87
Harding, James Marshall 1808, 28
Harding, James R., 117
Harding, James W., 29
Harding, James W. 1844, 73
Harding, Jane 1825, 144
Harding, Janet, 116
Harding, Janet M., 115
Harding, Jean, 85, 115
Harding, Jeanette Crighton 1886, 140
Harding, Jeanne, 31
Harding, Jessica 1992, 32
Harding, Jessie May 1881, 135
Harding, John, 1, 3, 8, 31, 142
Harding, John 1683, 1
Harding, John 1718, 5
Harding, John 1792, 129
Harding, John B. 1862, Reverend, 126
Harding, John C., Jr., 144
Harding, John E. 1863, 99, 100
Harding, John Edgar, 144
Harding, John Edward 1899, 115
Harding, John Edward, Jr., 116
Harding, John H., 107
Harding, John H. m/1828, 144
Harding, John L, Jr. 1829, 30

Harding, John Lackland 1780, 3, 27
Harding, John Maurice 1959, 89
Harding, John N. 1859, 130
Harding, John Randolph 1876, 90
Harding, John Robert 1839, 73
Harding, John Robert 1887, 100
Harding, John S. 1853, 144
Harding, John T. 1832, 118
Harding, John Thomas 1954, 86
Harding, John Thornley, 144
Harding, John W. 1789, 69, 73, 75, 83, 93
Harding, Joseph, 31, 114
Harding, Joseph 1822, 73, 75
Harding, Joseph 1857, 143
Harding, Joseph Emmitt 1903, 31
Harding, Joseph Marion 1917, 80
Harding, Josephine 1850, 139
Harding, Josephine I., 146
Harding, Josiah 1764, 7
Harding, Josiah 1790, 8
Harding, Josiah 1817, Doctor, 7, 22
Harding, Joyce, 117
Harding, Joyce Eileen 1944, 32
Harding, Julia A. 1845, 131
Harding, Julia Ann, 141
Harding, Julia Ann 1824, 131
Harding, Julia Halley, 29
Harding, Julia V., 116
Harding, Kammerer 1896, 144
Harding, Kate 1863, 24
Harding, Katherine 1819, 70
Harding, Kathleen, 31
Harding, Kathy, 114
Harding, Katie M. 1895, 100
Harding, Kay H. 1934, 134
Harding, Kenneth L., 116
Harding, Keturah m/1824, 144
Harding, Keziah, 11
Harding, L. (fem), 145
Harding, Laura, 113
Harding, Laura M. 1866, 112
Harding, Laura Virginia 1867, 120
Harding, Lawrence Edgar 1886, 84
Harding, Lee, 29
Harding, Lee m/1938, 144
Harding, Lee Nathaniel, 144
Harding, Lewis, 3, 125
Harding, Lewis 1722, 5
Harding, Lewis D. m/1870, 132
Harding, Lewis Montgomery 1890, 91
Harding, Lewis R., 141
Harding, Lewis Ridgely 1816, 126
Harding, Lita Joan, 116
Harding, Lizzie 1865, 24
Harding, Lloyd F. 1794, 107, 110
Harding, Lloyd Joseph 1840, 113
Harding, Lohadian 1823, 137
Harding, Lois June 1933, 81
Harding, Lorraine E., 105
Harding, Lottie Charlotte 1893, 85
Harding, Lottie Mae 1887, 141
Harding, Lottie S. 1885, 74
Harding, Louis Willoughby 1874, 121
Harding, Louisa, 30
Harding, Louise, 85
Harding, Lowell S. 1894, 143
Harding, Lucinda Catherine 1847, 129
Harding, Lucy 1724, 5
Harding, Lucy 1854, 24
Harding, Lucy Rice 1848, 25
Harding, Lula Gertrude 1884, 77
Harding, Lynn, 135
Harding, M. E. 1844, 144
Harding, Mabel Selina 1901, 89
Harding, Mable G. 1867, 144
Harding, Margaret, 31
Harding, Margaret 1832, 128
Harding, Margaret Ann, 131
Harding, Margaret Eleanor, 31

Harding, Margaret Elizabeth 1844, 83
Harding, Margaret J. 1857, 120
Harding, Margaret Louisa Shepherd 1808, 25
Harding, Margaret Rebecca 1882, 91
Harding, Margery, 3
Harding, Margery 1774, 9
Harding, Margery Lackland 1807, 25
Harding, Margie M. 1898, 145
Harding, Maria Louisa 1839, 30
Harding, Marian Sands 1861, 24
Harding, Marie Ruth 1893, 141
Harding, Marion M'liss 1912, 89
Harding, Marlene Sue 1948, 88
Harding, Marsha Ann 1953, 74
Harding, Marshall Fleming 1851, 29
Harding, Marshall Thomas 1875, 74
Harding, Marshall Thomas 1913, 74
Harding, Marshall Thomas, III 1955, 74
Harding, Martha B. 1870, 119, 120
Harding, Martha C., 105
Harding, Martha Matilda 1844, 139
Harding, Marvel Louise 1909, 80
Harding, Mary, 8, 9, 31, 132
Harding, Mary 1715, 5
Harding, Mary 1778, 9
Harding, Mary 1810, 69
Harding, Mary 1826, 23
Harding, Mary 1837, 119
Harding, Mary A. 1816, 12
Harding, Mary A. R. 1813, 125
Harding, Mary Ada 1879, 140
Harding, Mary Ann, 126
Harding, Mary Ann 1805, 25
Harding, Mary D., 90
Harding, Mary E., 145
Harding, Mary E. 1845, 30
Harding, Mary E. 1877, 113
Harding, Mary Elizabeth, 9
Harding, Mary Elizabeth 1842, 137
Harding, Mary Ellen 1837, 133
Harding, Mary Ellen 1909, 116
Harding, Mary Grace 1875, 28
Harding, Mary Jane 1839, 131
Harding, Mary Jane 1927, 145
Harding, Mary Laurette 1880, 140
Harding, Mary M., 104
Harding, Mary m/1830, 27
Harding, Mary Margaret 1890, 31
Harding, Mary V. 1846, 74
Harding, Mary V. 1858, 24
Harding, Mary Virginia 1836, 113
Harding, Mary Virginia 1850, 78
Harding, Maude, 29
Harding, Maude Irene 1882, 81
Harding, Maurice Lee 1935, 89
Harding, May Lydia 1874, 74
Harding, Maybel 1901, 145
Harding, Melissa, 103
Harding, Melvin Randolph 1884, 140
Harding, Melvin Woodrow 1924, 116
Harding, Merle, 103
Harding, Michael Eugene 1935, 145
Harding, Milan E., 85
Harding, Mildred Irene 1910, 87
Harding, Mildred L., 86
Harding, Millicent, 3
Harding, Milton Bentley 1880, 74
Harding, Minerva J. 1848, 139
Harding, Minnie, 29
Harding, Mollie A. 1848, 112
Harding, Mollie W. 1883, 74
Harding, Montella Roby, 140

Harding, Myrtle 1885, 113
Harding, Myrtle M. 1896, 85
Harding, N. B., 145
Harding, N. M. 1871, 133
Harding, Nancy Marie, 117
Harding, Nathan, 7
Harding, Nettie Mae 1891, 85
Harding, Nicholas 1872, 99
Harding, Nimrod 1813, 29
Harding, Norman Bruce 1812, 29
Harding, Norman L., 145
Harding, Norman Leo 1891, 145
Harding, Oliver P. 1822, 130
Harding, Ophelia Neal 1929, 117
Harding, Patricia Lynn 1956, 89
Harding, Paul D., 104
Harding, Paul D., Jr., 104
Harding, Pearl, 117
Harding, Pearl Nathalie 1884, 82
Harding, Peggy, 31
Harding, Pepsi, 103
Harding, Peyton 1792, 145
Harding, Philip, 132
Harding, Philip 1780, 9
Harding, Philip 1794, 127
Harding, Philip Thomas, 9
Harding, Priscilla Ann, 115
Harding, Raymond Whitney 1899, 103
Harding, Rebecca, 7
Harding, Rebecca R., 107
Harding, Regina Connelly, 120
Harding, Rena P. 1872, 142
Harding, Rezin, 3
Harding, Richard, 31
Harding, Richard A. 1803, 118
Harding, Richard m/1824, 145
Harding, Richard N. 1840, 118
Harding, Richard Thomas 1891, 141
Harding, Richard, Jr., 31
Harding, Robert 1891, 135
Harding, Robert Brawner 1940, 104
Harding, Robert Donald 1891, 103
Harding, Robert Henry 1825, 119
Harding, Robert L., 116
Harding, Robert Lee 1914, 145
Harding, Robert Mervin, 145
Harding, Roberta C. 1889, 120
Harding, Robin 1967, 32
Harding, Roger 1799, 25
Harding, Rose, 31
Harding, Ruby 1896, 99
Harding, Russell 1910, 87
Harding, Ruth, 85, 126
Harding, Ruth D., 117
Harding, Samuel Herbert 1873, 73, 145
Harding, Samuel Noah 1844, 73
Harding, Samuel R. 1812, 69, 73
Harding, Samuel R. 1839, 135
Harding, Samuel S. 1911, 145
Harding, Samuel Thomas 1858, 140
Harding, Sandra Lee 1958, 89
Harding, Sarah, 9
Harding, Sarah 1782, 125
Harding, Sarah 1793, 69
Harding, Sarah 1825, 73
Harding, Sarah Ann m/1834, 132
Harding, Sarah Catherine 1860, 120, 121
Harding, Sarah E. 1837, 131
Harding, Sarah F. 1849, 74
Harding, Sarah F. 1878, 73
Harding, Sarah Frances 1853, 78
Harding, Sharon Regenia, 117
Harding, Shirley, 117
Harding, Solomon, 131
Harding, Solomon E. d/1966, 145
Harding, Somerville 1848, 76
Harding, Sophia 1794, 110
Harding, Stanley Arthur 1911, 88
Harding, Steven Craig 1950, 88

Heeter, Lydia, 49
Heeter, Marion Alberta 1848, 49
Heeter, Vandelia 1855, 51
Heffiner, Minnie, 116
Heim, Lelia G. 1886, 104
Heise, America, 25
Helm, Eric Christian, 97
Helmick, Kevin Wayne, 104
Helmick, Kyle Wayne 1994, 104
Henderson, Ann 1860, 62
Henderson, Anna 1860, 61
Henderson, John 1856, 61, 62
Henderson, William 1878, 61
Henry, Bertha 1897, 49
*Hermitage*, 33, 38, 39
Herndon, Miranda, 39
Hershey, Donald J., 59
Hershey, No given name, 58
Hershey, Richard M., 59
Hilton, William P., 56
Hitz, Isabel Perry 1946, 46
Hitz, No given name, 46
Hobbs, Claude, 82
Hobbs, Gary William 1973, 82
Hobbs, Leonard 1914, 82
Hobbs, Michael Richard 1970, 82
Hobbs, Richard Eldon 1947, 82
Hobbs, Sandra Elaine 1941, 82
Hodson, Grace 1873, 102
Hoffler, Virginia, 116
Hoffman, William O., 130
Holland, Nathan, 11
Holland, Nathaniel, 1
Homa, Rock, 146
Hopkins, Adella M. 1880, 79
Hopkins, Haywood 1883, 78
Hopkins, Hiram W. 1849, 78
Hopkins, Mary E. 1880, 78
Hopkins, Samuel 1823, 79
Hopkins, Samuel Jefferson 1847, 78
Hoskinson, No given name, 20
Howard, Drusilla 1813, 112
Howard, Eleanor V. 1905, 101
Howard, Henrietta 1820, 118
Howard, Leonard 1799, 112
Howard, Leonard H. 1855, 112
Howard, Linwood 1874, 101
Howard, Mary Ann 1848, 112, 113
Howard, Mary Ellen, 113
Howard, Norman, 104
Howard, Roberta 1852, 112
Howard, Ruhama, 107
Hranicky, George Joseph, 64
Hranicky, Justine Claire 1957, 64
Hranicky, Kenneth Bede 1961, 64
Hranicky, Teresa Anne 1956, 64
Hranicky, Thomas Jerome 1958, 64
Hughes, No given name, 95, 114
Hughes, Rupert, 56
Hunt, Thomas H., Colonel, 30
Husband, No given name, 51
Hutson, Colin, 47
Iager, Henry Aaron, 140
Iager, Louisa Caroline 1858, 139
Iglehart, Helen Augusta, 73
Iglehart, Isaac 1800, 74
Iglehart, William W., 74
Inscoe, Donald Merrell 1966, 85
Inscoe, Garnett DeWitt, Jr., 85
Inscoe, Lawrence Mead 1958, 85
Inscoe, Rebecca Lee 1960, 85
Inscoe, Virginia Bell, 78
Irvine, Laura 1963, 44
Irvine, Margaret Lee 1961, 44
Irvine, Samuel John, III 1933, 44
Irvine, Samuel John, IV 1956, 44
Irvine, William Bruce 1959, 44
Jackson, Craven, Dr., 40
Jaeger, Margaret, 141
James, Horatio 1796, 13
Jamison, Aimee E., 112
Jamison, Alexander F. 1804, 109, 110

Marchesani, Dina, 32
Marchesani, Jay, 32
Marchesani, Nikki, 32
Marchesani, Richard, 32
Marchesani, Richard, Jr., 32
Markell, George, 28
Marlow, Mary Gertrude 1891, 94
Marlowe, George M., 41
Marrow, Harry, 85
Marrow, Milan H., 85
Marshall, Eleanor, 27
Marshall, James, 27
Marth, Wilbur Augustus, 90
Mathews, Charles H., 52
Mathews, Clarence H. 1889, 52
Matthews, Barbara Anne 1931, 64
Matthews, John Barry 1933, 64
Matthews, John Barry, Jr. 1957, 64
Matthews, Joseph Oscar 1901, 64
Matthews, Joseph Oscar, Jr. 1925, 64
Matthews, Margaret Keane 1958, 64
Matthews, Mary Claire 1924, 64
Matthews, Steven Kennedy, 64
Matthews, Susan Fisher 1959, 64
McAvoy, Mary E., 57
McBrian, No given name, 103
McCaffrey, Aloysius B. 1837, 129
McCaffrey, Michael 1791, 129
McCarthy, Denis, 30
McCarthy, Mary Ignatius, 30
McCarthy, Mary Margaret, 30
McClellan, L. Gladys, 58
McCrossin, Mary A. 1848, 56
McElfresh, Arianna 1828, 126
McElfresh, John Hammond 1796, Colonel, 126
McNulty, Elizabeth Lochner, 44
Mealy, Lydia, 127
Mealy, Milton, 127
Meredith, John A., 129
Michely, Elizabeth Catherine, 126
Miles, Thomas, 33
Miller, Charles, 10
Miller, J. Marshall, 132
Miller, Jan, 96
Miller, John Henry, 56
Milstead, Dora E. 1895, 138
Milstead, Lester L. 1899, 138
Milstead, No given name, 139
Milstead, Thomas L. 1871, 138
Milstead, Vetrice I. 1894, 138
Minyard, Bartow David, 48
Minyard, James Lamar 1932, 47
Minyard, Perry Lamar 1964, 48
Mollock, Gerald Chester, 90
Monast, Naomie Natalie, 39
Montgomery, Nellie, 90
Moore, Ada R. 1873, 86
Moore, Annie T. 1855, 72
Moore, Benjamin, 70
Moore, Charles 1854, 72
Moore, Charles W. 1871, 70
Moore, Donald, 136
Moore, Elias 1820, 70
Moore, Elizabeth A. 1866, 70
Moore, Elizabeth J. 1824, 75
Moore, Ellen 1856, 72
Moore, Evelyn 1908, 135
Moore, Isaac 1853, 72
Moore, Joseph 1914, 136
Moore, Joseph Pigman 1839, 135
Moore, Lester D. 1845, 144
Moore, Letitia J. 1858, 135
Moore, Mary 1851, 72
Moore, Rebecca 1856, 72
Moore, Robert, 136
Moore, Samuel Townsend 1891, 135
Moore, Sarah Ann 1849, 70
Moore, Sarah E. 1788, 69, 73, 75, 83, 93
Moore, Sarah F. 1842, 70
Morgan, Elaine Lillian 1926, 29

Morgan, James Littleton 1894, 29
Morgan, James Littleton, Jr. 1928, 29
Morgan, Robert, 121
Morris, Andrew Madison 1991, 67
Morris, Carl, 88
Morris, Harold Clayton 1923, 67
Morris, John Patrick 1954, 66
Morris, Joseph Guy 1989, 67
Morris, Percy C., 72
Moubray, Anne Stedman 1923, 81
Mullican, Barzilla Franklin 1833, 77
Mullican, Grace C. 1897, 102
Mullican, Mamie, 103
Mullican, Sarah F., 103
Mullican, William H., 143
Mullican, William Howard 1866, 77
Mullins, Foyster, 29
Murdock, John, Colonel, 33
Murphy, Emmett G., 22
Murphy, Mary, 8
Murphy, Mary Alice, 22
Murphy, Nancy, 22
Murphy, Patricia, 22
Murphy, Philip, 8
Murphy, Susan, 22
Murphy, Teresa, 22
Murry, Edward, 30
Mussetter, Charles F. 1834, 127
Mussetter, Jane 1840, 127
Mussetter, John 1836, 127
Mussetter, Lewis 1836, 127
Mussetter, Margaret 1804, 127
Mussetter, Michael 1843, 127
Mussetter, Philip 1798, 127
Mussetter, Sarah 1838, 127
Myers, Belinda E. 1829, 130
Myers, Maggie, 84
Myers, Margaret Elizabeth 1844, 83
Nash, Isabelle, 45
Nash, Minnie Lucile 1886, 45
Nash, Minnie Pappin 1886, 45
Neff, Gertrude, 90
Negro, Bambo, 33
Negro, Christy Ann, 36
Negro, Fann, 33
Negro, Gim, 35
Negro, Mark, 33
Negro, Ned, 33
Negro, Sauny, 33
Negro, Simon, 33
Nelson, No given name, 115
Neuenhahan, Florence, 32
Nicholson, Nellie, 121
Niles, Catherine, 38
Nivert, Edward Joseph 1947, 66
Nivert, Frank John 1915, 66
Nivert, Frank John, Jr. 1942, 66
Nivert, Mary Catherine 1944, 66
Noland, Agnes M. 1828, 19
Noland, Ann Butler 1824, 18
Noland, Anna Butler, 22
Noland, Dade, 14
Noland, Dade P. 1780, 15
Noland, Eleanor, 16
Noland, Fanny 1838, 22
Noland, James C. 1831, 19
Noland, Jane Elizabeth 1822, 16
Noland, Lloyd, 16
Noland, Maria 1832, 18
Noland, Mary Caroline 1833, 19
Noland, Mary Ellen, 22
Noland, Samuel, 16
Noland, Samuel S., 22
Noland, Thomas, 16
Noland, Thomas Edward 1826, 18
Norris, Hannah 1793, 129
Norris, No given name, 40
*Norris' Purchase*, 131
Norton, Cody, 96
Norton, Heather, 96
Norton, Jack, 96
Norton, Jerry, 96

Norton, Jerry, Jr., 96
Norton, Kelly, 96
Norton, Luke, 96
Norton, Rebecca, 96
Oden, Henry, 139
O'Donnohue, Dennis, 30
Offutt, Amy Cloud 1795, 48, 53
Offutt, Andrew, 19
Offutt, Catherine, 19
Offutt, Mary A., 52
Ogaard, Anthony 1954, 64
Ogaard, Elizabeth Jeanne 1951, 64
Ogaard, Helen Cecilia 1953, 64
Ogaard, Mary Caron Anne 1956, 64
Ogaard, Yves Joseph 1920, 64
Ogle, James, Sr., 29
Ogle, Joseph, 4
Ogle, Maria Ann 1814, 29
Ogle, Mary 1783, 30
Oglesbee, Kenneth, 114
O'Keefe, Bernice Elizabeth 1917, 90
O'Keefe, Curtis William 1969, 82
O'Keefe, Dennis Robert 1965, 82
O'Keefe, Douglas William 1912, 90
O'Keefe, Gertrude Marie 1906, 90
O'Keefe, Granville Jackson 1908, 90
O'Keefe, Russell Harding 1914, 90
O'Keefe, William 1871, 90
O'Keefe, William Robert, 82
O'Neal, Lucille Yvonne 1936, 64
Osborne, Grace, 50
Osmond, Aubrey 1891, 54
Osmond, Franklin J. 1895, 54
Osmund, Alcestra 1874, 55
Osmund, Belle Perry 1884, 55
Osmund, Benjamin 1868, 54
Osmund, Frances 1879, 55
Osmund, Inez 1877, 55
Osmund, Julian 1837, 54
Osmund, Julian E. 1866, 54
Osmund, Lelia Rhoda 1871, 54
Osmund, Mary L. 1870, 54
Osmund, Rhoda 1871, 54
Osthaus, Mabel E., 146
Owen, Ann, 11
Owen, Edward, 5
Owen, Edward 1763, 11
Owen, Eleanor, 11
Owen, Elizabeth, 11
Owen, Keziah, 2
Owen, Lawrence, 5
Owen, Mary, 11
Owen, Octavia, 11
Owen, Robert, 1, 11
Owen, Washington, 11
Owens, Emily 1818, 73
Owens, Mercy Ann, 69, 99
Parker, Harry George, 40
Parker, Mary 1782, 3
Parks, Ella May 1890, 80
Parks, George Washington, 80
Parsley, Edgar 1874, 95
Parson, Joan 1941, 82
Parsons, Mahala C., 28
Pate, Ethel May, 21
Patton, No given name, 91
Payne, No given name, 117
Payne, Susan Penn, 10
*Peace and Plenty*, 129, 131
Pearce, James, 38
Pearce, Maria 1832, 18
Pearce, William C., 18
Penn, Edward 1839, 143
Penn, Ruth Lillian, 88
Perrell, William, 104
Perry, Albert A. 1879, 51
Perry, Alice Emma 1917, 47
Perry, Althea 1865, 39
Perry, Alverda 1852, 40
Perry, Amanda 1859, 53
Perry, Amanda M. 1840, 40
Perry, Amelia 1839, 36

Perry, America 1871, 42
Perry, America Ann 1899, 41
Perry, Ann 1958, 41
Perry, Aquilina Maria 1822, 40
Perry, Arcadia Lee 1856, 41
Perry, Arthur Lee 1897, 53
Perry, Augustus Emory 1820, 37
Perry, Barbara 1860, 53
Perry, Basil Magruder, 36
Perry, Benjamin 1711, 33, 34
Perry, Benjamin 1785, 34
Perry, Benjamin 1874, 42
Perry, Benjamin Branham 1859, 39
Perry, Benjamin Cissell 1881, 45
Perry, Benjamin E. 1840, 38
Perry, Benjamin Franklin 1817, 36
Perry, Benjamin Joseph 1803, 36
Perry, Benjamin Waters, 39
Perry, Benjamin Waters 1812, 39
Perry, Bernard Clay 1885, 51
Perry, Caroline 1801, 38
Perry, Caroline Eliza 1808, 39
Perry, Caroline R. 1832, 36
Perry, Caroline Seay 1903, 42
Perry, Catherine, 38
Perry, Cecil Pappin 1914, 46
Perry, Charles Alexander 1818, 40
Perry, Charles Alexander 1901, 41
Perry, Charles Alexander, III 1953, 41
Perry, Charles Alexander, Jr. 1849, 40
Perry, Charles Alexander, Jr. 1928, 41
Perry, Charles d/1883, 37
Perry, Charles Wesley 1831, 38
Perry, Christiana m/1806, 38
Perry, Cora 1881, 50
Perry, Daniel Joseph 1963, 41
Perry, Dora Elva 1925, 49
Perry, Dorothy Ann 1829, 40
Perry, Eden T. d/1829, 37
Perry, Edgar Reed 1871, 49
Perry, Edmund 1806, 39
Perry, Edwin D. 1842, 38
Perry, Elbert 1782, 33, 48, 52
Perry, Elbert 1815, 34, 52
Perry, Elbert, Jr. 1861, 53
Perry, Eleanor 1855, 51
Perry, Eleanora 1810, 33
Perry, Eleanora Columbia 1816, 34
Perry, Elias 1788, 37, 39, 40
Perry, Elias Harding 1819, 40
Perry, Elizabeth 1803, 38
Perry, Elizabeth Ann 1804, 39
Perry, Elizabeth Eleanor 1895, 53
Perry, Elizabeth Harding 1803, 34
Perry, Elvira H. 1828, 40
Perry, Emma E. 1881, 46
Perry, Erasmus 1760, 33, 39
Perry, Erasmus 1806, 33, 48
Perry, Erasmus 1809, 35
Perry, Erasmus 1810, 39
Perry, Erasmus, Jr. 1793, 37, 42
Perry, Erasmus, Jr. 1858, 51
Perry, Florence 1860, 41
Perry, Florence 1900, 41
Perry, Frank 1858, 37
Perry, Gassaway 1787, 36
Perry, Gertrude Ruth, 51
Perry, Guy Rayhue 1900, 50
Perry, Hannah Bertha 1889, 51
Perry, Henry Clay F. 1852, 51
Perry, Henry Polkinhorn 1886, 48
Perry, Horace M. 1907, 51
Perry, Isabel Tracy 1912, 46
Perry, James 1841, 36
Perry, James Emory 1835, 38
Perry, James William 1826, 40
Perry, James Wilson d/1809, 7
Perry, Jane B. H., 50
Perry, John 1854, 52
Perry, John Augustus 1815, 40
Perry, John Elias 1870, 41

Poole, Thomas B. 1878, 139
Porfido, Frank, 22
Pose, Pierre, 46
Powell, No given name, 120
Powell, R. M., 56
Powers, James, 107
Prescott, Catherine Carter 1928, 48
Prescott, William H., 48
Price, David Joseph 1943, 48
Price, Frank Leib, 48
Price, No given name, 25
Pritchard, Charlotte Roby, 89
*Prospect Hall*, 45
Pumphrey, No given name, 117
Purvis, Emily 1863, 146
Purvis, William L. 1860, 146
Queen, Ellen R. 1834, 12
Rabbitt, John, 56
Ray, Effie Riggs 1887, 82
Ray, No given name, 72
Raynes, Bessie, 86
Raynolds, Nathan Hosea 1845, 75
Reed, Philip, 55
Reffitt, Selby P., 56
*Refuse*, 4
Reil, Lawrence, 31
Remington, Georgia 1845, 23
Reynolds, Josephine Geraldine 1842, 75
Rice, Clara E. 1852, 132
Rice, Elizabeth Higgason 1817, 25
Rice, George 1794, 30
Rich, Wilmer, 95
Richardson, Charles J. 1892, 72
Richardson, Clyde, 56
Richardson, Florence A. 1898, 72
Richardson, Gladys J., 72
Richardson, Lula Roberta 1901, 72
Richardson, Maude V. 1890, 71
Richardson, No given name, 139
Richardson, R. Milton, 72
Richardson, Robert J. T. 1858, 71
Richardson, Sarah Ethel 1895, 72
Richardson, Walter, 74
Ricketts, Bessie E. 1887, 122
Ricketts, David W., 63
Ricketts, Dorothy E., 123
Ricketts, Effie E. 1888, 122
Ricketts, Eugene E., Jr., 123
Ricketts, Eugene Washington 1898, 123
Ricketts, Frances E., 122
Ricketts, Frances E. 1894, 123
Ricketts, Francis E., 61
Ricketts, Katherine E. 1890, 122
Ricketts, Mary E. 1885, 121
Ricketts, Mildred Elizabeth, 90
Ricketts, Richard Edward 1829, 120, 121
Ricketts, Roberta Jane 1858, 120
Ricketts, Ulysses Magruder 1856, 121
Ridgely, Sarah 1782, 125
Ridgely, William, 125
Ridgeway, Margery, 5
Riggs, Nancy, 104
Riggs, No given name, 85
Riley, Frank C., 56
Riley, William R., 24
Robb, Adam, 15
Robb, Catherine Ann 1792, 12
*Robert's Store*, 46
Roberts, Eliza Ann, 28
Robertson, David Charles 1923, 49
Robertson, Joan Elizabeth 1947, 50
Roby, Carrie Frank 1885, 94
Roby, Edward Haslup 1879, 89
Roby, Marion Elizabeth 1905, 89
Rohland, Jo Ann, 82
Roles, Isaac, 39
Rolison, Harriet 1837, 54
Rosal, Clara E. 1910, 84

Thrift, Agnes Eugenia 1877, 56
Thrift, Charles Henry 1836, 56
Thrift, Elizabeth Jane 1828, 63
Tighe, Annie Catherine 1859, 135
Tighe, Peter 1891, 135
Tombes, Averett Snead, 42
Tombes, Robert McFarland, 42
Tombes, Thomas Hamilton, 42
Townsend, Lacey 1858, 135
Trail, Anna Mary 1859, 126
Trail, Charles Bayard 1857, 127
Trail, Charles Edward 1825, Colonel, 126
Trail, Christian Anne 1826, 120, 121
Trail, Elisha, 107
Truex, Aubrey Palmer 1902, 42
Truex, Eldone Hamilton 1896, 42
Truex, Harvey, 42
Truex, Rachel 1899, 42
Tucker, Benjamin C. 1852, 77
Tucker, Richard 1808, 76
Tucker, Susan Jane 1848, 76
Turner, Alice Joyce 1920, 82
Turner, Archibald Stirling 1883, 82
Turner, Bertie Anne Irene 1946, 81
Turner, Carrie Virginia 1873, 136
Turner, Carroll Wayne 1940, 81, 82
Turner, Charles Colin 1942, 81
Turner, Colin Harding 1920, 81
Turner, Edith Arlene 1919, 81, 82
Turner, Gary Lee 1963, 82
Turner, Harry Alonzo 1878, 81
Turner, Harry Alonzo, III 1942, 81
Turner, Harry Alonzo, Jr. 1912, 81
Turner, James Fletcher 1850, 81, 82
Turner, Kathy Irene 1961, 82
Turner, Larry Lee 1965, 82
Turner, Mitchell Blair Thomas 1953, 81
Turner, Robert Lee 1926, 82
Turner, Stirling Carroll 1914, 81, 82
Turner, Sylvia Yvonne 1937, 81, 82
Turner, Walter Perry 1945, 81
Upshall, Harry, Doctor, 95
Valdenar, Francis 1797, 23
Valdenar, Frank, III, 85
Valdenar, Mary Virginia 1826, 23
Van Horn, Alice V. 1869, 71
Van Horn, Dorothy Lee, 90
Van Horn, Jacob 1844, 70
Van Horn, Martha E. 1867, 71
Vernon, Catherine, 20
Viett, Margaret E., 123
Vinson, Peyton D., 53
Vitt, Michael Darrin, 97
Vitt, Taylor Elizabeth, 97
Wadford, Clinton Franklin, 87
Wainscott, No given name, 85
Walker, Sarah F. Mullican, 103
Wallick, Charles Hewlett, 140
Walton, Shirlie Belle 1933, 89
Wargowski, Beatrice, 146
Waters, Anne, 39
Waters, Anne 1758, 36
Waters, Aquilina 1786, 39, 40
Waters, Benjamin 1756, 36, 39
Waters, Delilah Elizabeth 1785, 36
Waters, John, 42
Waters, Margaret Bell 1849, 42
Watkins, Mary E. 1847, 100
Watson, Catherine, 58
Watson, Edward, 58
Watson, Edward P., 58
Watson, Michael, 135
*Wayman's Purchase*, 107
Weaver, Alice Emma 1886, 46

Wilson, Frank Hallowell 1889, 95, 96
Wilson, Frank William, 97
Wilson, Franklin Littleton 1857, 95, 96
Wilson, Grace Kathryn 1903, 95
Wilson, Horace 1850, 93
Wilson, Jennie, 39
Wilson, John, 93
Wilson, John Henry 1855, 93
Wilson, John W., 94
Wilson, John Woodrow, 96
Wilson, Juanita, 94
Wilson, Kenneth, 96
Wilson, Laura Frances 1864, 95
Wilson, Lee Jennings, 95
Wilson, Letitia May, 94
Wilson, Lottie Marie 1900, 95
Wilson, Margaret Claretta 1881, 95
Wilson, Margaret Ella 1862, 95
Wilson, Mary Catherine 1853, 93
Wilson, Mildred Audrey 1917, 94
Wilson, Milton, 10
Wilson, No given name, 138
Wilson, Norman Leslie 1892, 95
Wilson, Raphael, 96
Wilson, Roy Haywood 1890, 94
Wilson, Roy Lee, 94
Wilson, Sarah Elizabeth 1851, 93
Wilson, Silas Randolph 1859, 95
Wilson, Sophy M. 1870, 96
Wilson, Talmadge Duane, 94
Wilson, Thelma Elizabeth, 94
Wilson, Virgie M. 1893, 95
Wilson, William Adolphus 1849, 93
Wilson, William Franklin 1817, 93
Wilson, William Henry 1887, 94
Wilson, William Leslie, 94
Winters, Sarah, 4
Wolfe, George, 28
Wolfe, Mary E. 1843, 28, 30
Woodward, Arthur Fletchall 1920, 136
Woodward, Arthur Fletchall, Jr. 1951, 137
Woodward, Charles William 1895, 136
Woodward, Diane Fletchall 1950, 137
Woodward, Kathy Lemoine 1949, 137
Woodward, Nancy Harding 1948, 136
Woodward, William Bryan, 81
Wootton, No given name, 91
Works, Alisa, 32
Works, Homer, 32
Works, Larry, 32
Wrenn, Louis Isaac 1868, 80
Wright, Clarence Edward, 89
Wright, Clarence Herbert, 141
Wright, Rose Anna, 48
Wright, Shelva Jean 1940, 135
Wright, William J., 72
Wynkoop, No given name, 102
Wynkoop, Susan, 134
Yates, John Charles, 20
Young, Lester, 74
Young, Martha Ann 1827, 40
Young, William P., Dr., 37
Youngjohns, Marian Alicia 1954, 47
Youngjohns, Richard Paxson 1931, 47
Youngjohns, Stephanie Jane 1964, 47
Zimmerman, Ann Gould 1929, 41
Zimmerman, Arthur G., 41
Zimmerman, Bruce Alan, 97
Zimmerman, Garrett Alan, 97
Zimmerman, Janet Perry 1926, 41
Zimmerman, Noelle Lee, 97

Mr. Hurley is a ninth-generation descendant of Daniel Hurley, who immigrated to Talbot County, Md. in 1679 as an indentured servant. Discharged from the Navy in 1946 after serving as a bomb disposal specialist in the Marshall Islands Campaign, he has lived in Montgomery County, Maryland for more than fifty years, and writes primarily of county families, often based on personal contacts and, occasionally, as a distant relative of the family under study. He is a land surveyor, retired vice president of a major local building and development firm, former Gaithersburg City councilman, and has held numerous social and civic positions. He has two sons and seven grandchildren and, with his wife of nearly fifty years now in an Alzheimer's facility, lives alone in the town of thirty thousand that he helped build and develop, which contains a local park named in his honor. He is a prolific writer of genealogical works, having more than fifty books published by Heritage Books, Inc., and in 2001 was the recipient of the Norris Harris Prize from the Maryland Historical Society for the best compilation of genealogical source records in Maryland.